SPOOKY

Washington

SPOOKY
Washington

*Tales of Hauntings, Strange Happenings,
and Other Local Lore*

RETOLD BY S. E. SCHLOSSER

ILLUSTRATED BY PAUL G. HOFFMAN

Guilford, Connecticut

Text copyright © 2010 by S. E. Schlosser

Illustrations copyright © 2010 by Paul G. Hoffman

Project editor: David Legere
Text design/layout: Lisa Reneson, Two Sisters Design
Map: M. A. Dubé © Morris Book Publishing, LLC

Library of Congress Cataloging-in-Publication Data is available on file.

ISBN 978-0-7627-5126-6

Printed in the United States of America

10 9 8 7 6 5 4 3 2 1

For my family: David, Dena, Tim, Arlene, Hannah, Emma, Nathan, Ben, Deb, Gabe, Clare, Jack, Chris, Karen, Davey, and Aunt Mil.

For Mary Norris, Paul Hoffman, Erin Turner, Jess Haberman, and all the wonderful folks at Globe Pequot Press, with my thanks.

For Pam and Norm. And for Greg, with my thanks for the great stories and helpful hints you shared as I navigated my way around the San Juan islands.

Contents

MAP   x

INTRODUCTION   xiii

PART ONE: GHOST STORIES   1

1.   *The Phantom Grocer*   2
     SPOKANE

2.   *At the Market*   7
     SEATTLE

3.   *The Warning*   13
     CASCADE MOUNTAINS

4.   *I Am Your Brother*   18
     LEAVENWORTH

5.   *The Final Ride*   24
     KENT

6.   *The Extra Student*   30
     VANCOUVER

7.   *The Last Vigilante*   34
     ROCKFORD

8.   *The Rocking Chair*   40
     BELLINGHAM

9.   *Sailor's Revenge*   49
     PORT TOWNSEND

10. *Steak and Eggs*   57
     SPOKANE

11. *Has Anyone Seen My Cow?*   61
     STEILACOOMB

12. *The Mausoleum*   66
     SAN JUAN ISLANDS

13. *Get Out!*   74
     BREMERTON

PART TWO: POWERS OF DARKNESS AND LIGHT   79

14.   *Thirteen Steps*   80
      MALTBY

15.   *Tree Octopus*   87
      OLYMPIC PENINSULA

16.   *The Draug*   97
      POULSBO

17.   *Flying Saucers*   106
      MOUNT RAINIER

18.   *The Miser*   111
      TACOMA

19.   *Mountain Devils*   122
      MOUNT ST. HELENS

20.   *Bone Cleaner*   130
      DOUGLAS COUNTY

21.   *The Message*   136
      RICHLAND

22.   *Demon Man*   143
      YAKIMA

23.   *Soap*   150
      LAKE CRESCENT

24.   *The Wax Doll*   155
      WALLA WALLA

25.   *Beloved Woman*   165
      MOUNT ST. HELENS

26.   *Totem*   175
      SEATTLE

RESOURCES   195
ADDITIONAL CHAPTER   199
ABOUT THE AUTHOR   207
ABOUT THE ILLUSTRATOR   208

SPOOKY SITES . . .

1. Spokane
2. Seattle
3. Cascade Mountains
4. Leavenworth
5. Kent
6. Vancouver
7. Rockford
8. Bellingham
9. Port Townsend
10. Spokane
11. Steilacoomb
12. San Juan Islands
13. Bremerton

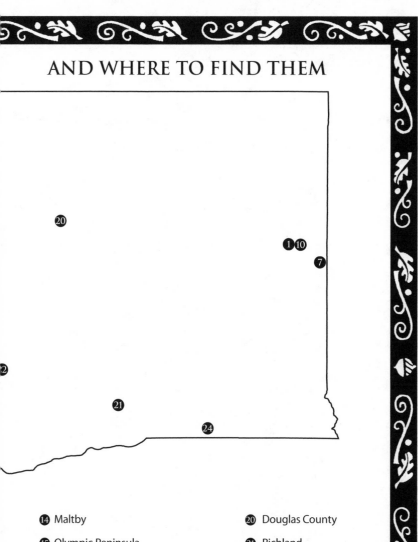

AND WHERE TO FIND THEM

⓮ Maltby

⓯ Olympic Peninsula

⓰ Poulsbo

⓱ Mount Rainier

⓲ Tacoma

⓳ Mount St. Helens

⓴ Douglas County

㉑ Richland

㉒ Yakima

㉓ Lake Crescent

㉔ Walla Walla

㉕ Mount St. Helens

㉖ Seattle

Introduction

For some reason, I kept expecting eastern Washington to be a flat place. So it came as quite a surprise when the SUV began turning sharp corners, dipping down into gullies and washes and coulees that appeared right out of the blue. I was driving along what looked—at first glance—to be a completely flat plateau. And suddenly, I was descending sharply into a dried riverbed. It was surreal.

My destination was Palouse Falls, which was supposed to be absolutely spectacular, according to the guidebooks. Personally, I was finding the surprising landscape around me—from its prairie grasses to the farms tucked into strange rocky cuts in the land—to be rather spectacular. So the falls must really be something, I imagined.

I put on my blinker and made the turn onto the road leading to the falls. As I did, a coyote shot out of the pasture to my right, galloped across the road, wriggled under a low fence, and trotted up the hill on my left. It had the slyest expression I had ever seen on an animal—like a cat caught with a canary in its mouth. The coyote paused halfway up the slope and turned to look at me. I pulled over at once, seized my camera, and started shooting photo after photo while it trotted to the top of the ridge and then disappeared over the other side. Of course, I mused as I headed back onto the road. This was the land of Coyote, the trickster-god (Totem). No wonder this was a place of surprises.

The biggest surprise lay in front of me. The driveway into the falls was just a dirt and gravel road. I parked in the lot, hearing thundering water and seeing mist rising from a huge gorge ahead of me. I walked to the viewing platform and gaped in amazement. Once again, a flat plateau was suddenly cut away, as if knocked off by a giant hand. The huge canyon in front of me had a lovely waterfall cascading out of the basalt wall about midway down the face of the cliff. To my right, the river flowed through a massive gorge torn willy-nilly out of the surrounding plateau. It was spectacular! Wow, Coyote! Look at what you did!

According to the signposts at Palouse Falls, glaciers creeping down from the north during the last ice age had dammed a great river and formed massive Lake Missoula, which was larger than any of the Great Lakes of today. The pressure of the water had eventually broken the ice dam, draining a lake that was more than two thousand feet in depth within forty-eight hours. Massive amounts of water had hurtled through eastern Washington with incredible, catastrophic force. The water had ripped through the basalt laid down by ancient volcanoes, cutting riverbeds and waterfalls, making deep channels in one place and leaving huge gravel beds in another. Where the water smashed against hard hillsides, massive bubble-tornados formed, drilling perfectly round holes into the rock. When the flood abated, the land was changed forever into the wonder known today as the Channeled Scablands.

By the time I reached Spokane—once home to a Phantom Grocer—I was completely in love with eastern Washington. From Walla Walla—where a witch once cast an evil spell on a missionary—to the farmland of the Palouse; and from Yakima—once home to an alien from outer space—to Grand Coulee, I found eastern Washington to be an amazing place (The Wax Doll, Demon Man). Not to mention a spooky one. And there was more to come.

As my SUV crossed the Cascades on the Northern Cascades Highway, I found myself gazing down at the amazing inland Salish Sea. Here was another kind of spectacular—from the massive Mount Rainier with its Flying Saucers and its buried treasure (The Miser) to the lovely rainforests of the Olympic Peninsula, full of strange, scary surprises (Soap) and creatures known only to cryptobiologists (Tree Octopus). I watched a gray whale spouting near Whidbey Island; I photographed seals basking near Roche Harbor with its haunted Mausoleum; and I roamed the haunted Pike Place Market in Seattle (At the Market). And I found myself just as much in love with western Washington as I was with its eastern counterpart.

The most moving place I visited was Mount St. Helens, which inspired two stories for this collection (Mountain Devils and Beloved Woman). Seeing firsthand the devastation of the 1980 volcanic eruption and the slow recovery of the mountain hit me harder than I expected. The memory of the shattered landscape lingers in my mind to this day.

Washington is a state of spectacular natural beauty and equally spectacular natural disasters. It is a state of warm, friendly people—and some downright spooky ghosts! I hope you grow to love it as much as I do. And the next time you are in the Channeled Scablands . . . give my best wishes to Coyote.

—*Sandy Schlosser*

PART ONE
Ghost Stories

The Phantom Grocer

SPOKANE

It was a stressful time for the newlywed couple. The Depression had hit hard, and the young husband was desperately seeking a job to support his new wife, without success. She had no training herself, and all the entry-level jobs for which she might qualify were snatched up as soon as they opened. They were living in eastern Washington, with no family or friends nearby to help them. And they weren't particularly religious, so they had no synagogue or church community to help them. They were too proud to accept charity, even if they had been.

Finally, the young husband decided to use his last few dollars to travel to Seattle and look for work. His wife didn't like this idea at all but said nothing in protest—even though she had just learned that she was carrying their first child. But there were no jobs in eastern Washington, so what else could her husband do? She didn't tell him about the baby. That would be more pressure than he could bear. She just hugged him goodbye and nodded tearfully when he told her that he'd arranged a line of credit with the local grocer while he was gone.

The young wife hated buying on credit, but the old man who owned the grocery was kind and never mentioned her growing debt. Instead, he chatted about local events and the weather. She learned from her neighbors that he was supporting several needy families in this way, which made her feel a little better about the situation.

The days were long and empty for the young wife. She kept the tiny house spotless, but her pregnancy made her increasingly ill, so she mostly stayed home. After two months, she reached the limit of the credit her husband had procured with the grocer. Feeling wretchedly sick and too proud to beg the grocer to extend her line of credit, she stretched out her meager supplies until she had nothing left, not even fuel for the stove. By then, she was so depressed that she huddled under the bedcovers for warmth and stayed there as much as possible, simply to keep from freezing to death.

Several miserable days had passed in this manner when she heard a knock. She was weak from hunger and shivering with cold, but she pulled herself out of bed and shuffled to the front door. When she opened it, no one was there. But on the stoop were two boxes full of groceries bearing the logo of the local store and enough fuel to last for the next month.

She fell to her knees, overwhelmed with gratitude. Her husband must have contacted the grocer to extend their credit. And—bless the man—he had delivered the supplies right to her door. With shaking hands, the young wife pulled the heavy boxes into the cold house and had her first meal in days, sitting on the floor by the front door.

She was very careful with the fuel and food, for winter was upon her, and she had to make the supplies last until her husband returned. But no matter how little she ate, the supplies dwindled away too quickly, until she had eaten every last morsel

THE PHANTOM GROCER

and used every scrap of fuel. She would have to go to the grocer in the morning and see if there was any more credit, she decided.

That night, she was seized by a great pain. Within a few minutes, she had lost the baby, and she lay ill in bed for several days afterward, unable to move farther than the tiny bathroom that stood right beside the bedroom. She was weak with pain and hunger and miserable in spirit when she heard a rat-a-tat-tat on the front door. She propped herself up against the pillows weakly, her heart springing up with hope. Was it her husband? No, he wouldn't knock. But the grocer would!

Wearily, she dragged herself to the door on hands and knees. She pulled herself upright on the doorknob, ashamed to appear before her visitor in such a bedraggled state but unable to do anything about it. She opened the door. Again, no one was there. But the expected supplies were on the stoop. She cried with relief as she pulled them inside and shut the door against the cold. Bless the grocer. Bless him and her husband, who was providing for her from afar.

Soon, the house was warm, and she was feeling better. The food helped her body heal, and within a couple of weeks, she was ready to venture out of doors. She was determined to go to the grocery and thank the proprietor who had delivered food to her doorstep when she needed it so desperately.

Donning her best hat and dress, she walked out into the fresh air of early spring and made her way slowly toward the store. To her astonishment, she found the shop locked and the windows papered over. The store was closed and obviously had been for some time. A woman passing by asked the young wife if she needed help. The young wife turned to her in some distress and asked about the grocer.

"Didn't you know?" the woman replied. "He died just before the new year. We've got to go all the way into downtown Spokane now to get supplies."

The young wife blanched and swayed when she heard the news. The woman, alarmed, asked if anything was wrong. The young wife shook her head, thanked the woman, and slowly began to walk home. The groceries had come from this store. She had recognized the boxes. And no one else in the area knew her troubles—indeed, she had no friends or family nearby at all. So who had delivered the groceries?

But she already knew by the prickling sensation along her arms and the back of her neck. There was only one person who could have known that she was quietly starving to death in her little house. The dead grocer. And by some miracle, he had kept faith with her husband, delivering groceries to his starving wife long after he himself had passed away.

A few days later, the husband returned home, without money but with seeds enough to start a garden. By the time the grocer's final gift had been used up, the couple had food coming in from their garden, and the husband had found part-time work that helped them through the rest of the Depression.

But the young wife knew she would never have survived if it hadn't been for the generosity of the phantom grocer of Spokane.

2

At the Market

SEATTLE

All day long, I'd been looking forward to a visit to Pike Place Market. My husband wasn't that interested in shopping, but he'd agreed to take me to the famous street market if I'd let him go charter fishing in the Puget Sound the next day. Seemed like a good deal to me!

We arrived after lunch at the main entrance to the marketplace, and I gaped like a little kid at all the colors and sounds. Even my husband got a kick out of seeing the market's many stalls and strolling musicians, as well as every type of product you could imagine hanging in doors and windows. Hawkers shouted out their wares to passersby. Smells of flour and cinnamon and newly baked bread wafted by on the wind, causing my nostrils to twitch and my husband to disappear. I was just getting worried when he reappeared with two fresh-baked cinnamon rolls in his hands.

We munched happily as we strolled through the crowds, as bright and colorful as the goods being sold. It was a lovely, sunny day, unusual in Seattle, where clouds and rain tend to dominate the weather. My husband pulled me into a nearby park to look at the totem poles standing proudly overlooking the sound. Then I pulled him back into the marketplace to search for the source of the wonderful flower bouquets being carried in the arms of many passing shoppers. My husband's pretty swift on the uptake, and a few minutes later I was happily strolling along with my own flower masterpiece cradled in my arms.

At this point in our meanderings, we hit a solid wall of people; far too many to be moving through the narrow space between the stalls. I stayed close to my husband as I was buffeted from side-to-side by passing men, women, and children. I got an elbow in the ribs at one point, and a very rude young person cursed at me when I stepped in his way. Then someone stepped on my foot with the heel of a boot just outside a jewelry stall. By the time we reached the end of the row, I was limping and cursing under my breath and as grumpy as all get-out.

My husband was in no better state. He hates crowds worse than I do. He guided me down a ramp to the lower level of the market and found a quiet corner near a gift shop where I could lurk with my flowers while he found us something to drink. My brave hero rushed back into the swirling, wall-to-wall crowd of shoppers and disappeared from view.

I pretended to browse the nearby stalls, moving slowly in my little backwater, nursing my lovely flowers and trying not to put too much weight on my throbbing foot. I wanted to get back the holiday mood I'd had when we entered the market, but it was hard to do with my side still hurting from the elbowing, and my temper still red-hot from the young man's cursing. If he'd been my son, he'd have ended up in his room for being so rude to an adult.

As I stood stewing, my eyes were caught by a tall, almost ethereal figure walking down the corridor in my direction. She was a striking Native American woman with long, dark braids reaching to her waist and a lovely native basket in her hands. She wore a shimmering dress that at first I took to be white, then realized was pink. Or was it lavender? It swirled gracefully around her, covered by an old shawl that had been lovingly preserved. It was the serenity of the woman's countenance amidst the chaos of the marketplace that caught my eye. Strangely, no one else in the crowded hallway seemed to notice her. Their eyes swerved away from her, though they unconsciously made way for her as she passed. She seemed to be part of the environment without actually interacting with it, and she looked neither left nor right as she walked the hallway.

The maiden passed right in front of me at that moment, and I realized two things at once. First, I saw that she was glowing with a faint, white light. Second, I realized that I could see the stall on the other side of the hall right through her body. My mouth dropped open so far I felt my jaw pop, and goose bumps ran up the length of my arms under their flowery burden.

A moment later, the ghostly maiden turned and walked right through a wall, vanishing before my eyes. Chills rippled underneath my skin, and I started shaking. I wasn't afraid. It was impossible to be afraid of someone so serene. But I felt horribly uneasy and distressed at the sight of something so . . . unnatural.

At that moment my husband appeared, holding two cold cans of soda. "Come on, honey, I found us a place to sit!" He caught my arm with his free hand and guided me out of the marketplace to a quiet bench overlooking the sound. He must have felt me shaking, because he kept peering anxiously down at me as we walked. Once we were seated, with the huge bouquet between us on the cool stone bench, and I'd had a few calming

AT THE MARKET

sips of soda, he asked me what was wrong. I told him at once about seeing the ghost of the Native American woman in the marketplace. I've always made it my policy to tell my husband everything that was happening in my life, and I wasn't about to make an exception now—even though he probably wouldn't believe me. Anyway, what I'd seen was so amazing and so surreal that I had to talk about it!

"It was so strange, seeing a ghost in a crowded hallway. And no one else seemed to notice her at all," I concluded. "Maybe I imagined the whole thing."

To my surprise, my husband shook his head. "I don't think you imagined it," he said. "Your story dovetails nicely with some rumors I've heard recently about Pike Place Market."

My eyes popped. "It does?"

"Yes, it does," he said, patting my hand comfortingly. "The ghost of an Indian maiden has been seen walking these hallways for decades. Sometimes she appears in the stalls, sometimes she walks through walls, and sometimes she wanders the hallways with a basket in her hands. Some people think she's the ghost of Princess Angeline, the daughter of Chief Seattle, who used to live in this city. Others think she was one of the women who sold baskets in the marketplace when it first opened. No one knows why her spirit still appears here. But you're not the first to have seen her. And you probably won't be the last!"

I sighed a little in relief, grateful that he believed my story and that I had some sort of explanation for what I'd seen. I rubbed the pink petals of a peony between my thumb and forefinger, enjoying the satiny texture of the flower as we sat in silence for a few minutes, pondering the imponderable. Finally, I shook myself all over, stood up, and picked up my flowers.

"Well, I guess I got my money's worth out of this visit to the market," I said.

"You sure did! Cinnamon rolls, soda pop, flowers, and a ghost," my husband said with a grin. "Come on, let's go get some dinner!"

Grabbing my free hand, he laced his fingers through mine and led me away from the supernatural and into the golden light of a late Seattle afternoon in spring.

3

The Warning

CASCADE MOUNTAINS

My brothers and I headed out for our hiking trip right after work on Friday. We were climbing up Three Fingers in the morning and wanted to get a head start on our climb, which would be challenging, to say the least. We were experienced climbers by now, having grown up in these parts. Our mother often said we were as surefooted as mountain goats, and she was right.

We parked our car near Boulder Creek, shouldered backpacks and axes, and started down the trail. As we hiked along, my brothers started joking about it being Friday the thirteenth, and I gave them a warning frown. I'd seen some strange things happen on such Fridays and didn't want them happening to me.

The sun had gone down and it was nearly ten o'clock when we came across a lean-to next to the trail. It was a perfect spot to settle for the night—so we did. Four bunks to choose from—luxury indeed! I shrugged out of my backpack, swung myself up into the top bunk, and found myself gazing through a crack in the roof of the old building. Through the tear in the roof, I could see the Milky Way glowing brightly in the beautiful, starry sky. Shifting a bit against my pillow, I could see mist rising over the ponds in the valley below.

It was a lovely night, but the sight of the mist gave me chills for some reason. I turned my eyes away and listened to the familiar banter between my brothers as they settled themselves into the two lower bunks. Soon, we were all asleep.

I'm not exactly sure what woke me. All I know is that my mind was suddenly alert, my arms crawling with chills, and my whole body stiff with fear. My ears strained for the slightest sound, but I heard nothing—not even the hoot of an owl or the rustle of night creatures in the underbrush. The silence around me was uncanny. I kept my eyes squeezed shut, as if I could keep the danger at bay if I didn't see it. But that was ridiculous. I took a deep breath. Heart thudding, every nerve in my body tingling, I opened my eyes. And found myself staring into the floating, softly glowing face of a man. Just a face. With no body attached. I gasped softly, my body going rigid with terror. The apparition appeared to be young—maybe twenty—with a couple days' growth of beard and the bluest eyes I'd ever seen. His skin was a sickly blue color too—as if he were very cold, and his nose and mouth were tightly drawn.

I had no idea what to do. Swallowing hard against a lump in my throat, I croaked: "Can I help you?" Instantly, the face vanished.

I drew in a sharp breath, as shocked by the face's disappearance as by its manifestation. I rubbed my shoulders and arms fiercely, as much to comfort myself as to get rid of the chills. Why had the spirit appeared to me? Was someone ill or in danger?

I finally managed to rub some life back into my body and felt my fear slowly drain away. I settled back against the pillow and pulled the blanket tight over me. Outside, I could hear the crickets resume their nightly chirping and little creatures returning to their pursuits. The uncanny silence was gone, and that must mean the spirit—whoever he was—would probably not return. I relaxed a bit but couldn't get back to sleep. Instead, I lay staring into the darkness, seeing the face over and over again in my mind and pondering the incident until dawn.

Over breakfast, I told my brothers all about the blue-eyed ghost-face I'd seen hovering above me. Predictably, they laughed. Said I was dreaming. I glared at them and described the face in detail—stunning blue eyes, stubble of beard, bluish skin, and pinched nose and mouth. They still didn't believe me. I guess it was an outlandish story, but I knew I hadn't dreamed the incident, and I said so.

Agreeing to disagree, the three of us headed out toward Three Fingers, enjoying the lovely weather and eager to make the climb. We were about seven miles into our route when we chanced across a ranger. He hailed us, and we went over to speak to him. He inquired about our route up the mountain. When we told him, he advised us to take a different path. That particular hike was still dangerous because of all the deep snow we'd had this past winter. He offered to show us a safer trail, and we accepted at once.

As we changed directions, the ranger told us that he'd been posted to this particular trail to intercept hikers like ourselves because of a recent accident. A few days earlier, a party of three had taken the very same trail we were climbing, and one of them had slipped and fallen into a crevice to his death.

My heart gave a strange thud when I heard his words, and the insides of my arms broke out with goose bumps. I whirled

THE WARNING

to face the ranger. "What did he look like?" I asked urgently. "The man who fell."

The ranger stopped walking and stared at me. My brothers slowed to a halt and turned to watch us.

"He wasn't pretty," the ranger said. The man had died on impact, and by the time the rescue crew had arrived, his body was a mess. The ranger was reluctant to continue, but I pressed him until he described the man as a twenty-year-old with a couple days' growth of beard and the bluest eyes he'd ever seen.

I drew in a deep, deep breath. Then I looked at my brothers. We'd started out on Friday the thirteenth, and the ghost of a dead man had appeared to me in the middle of the night. It was too much of a coincidence to ignore. And I saw from my brothers' expressions that they agreed.

There was a long pause, and then all three of us spoke at once, our words tumbling over each other as we told the ranger that we'd changed our minds. We'd climb the mountain another day. Bidding the man farewell, we headed for home, hiking right past our base camp at the lean-to and down toward the car.

It wasn't until we got back to my place that we learned that a huge avalanche had crashed down from the peak we intended to climb on Three Fingers, just a few hours after we turned for home. It had buried the trail we were hiking and everything on it. If we'd have kept going, we'd have been dead.

4

I Am Your Brother

LEAVENWORTH

Life was kind of rough for me that year. I was down and out, with no money in my pocket to speak of and no job. I had drifted to Spokane, but there wasn't anything for me there, so I rode the rails west, hoping to find something in Seattle.

Sounds nice and comfy, doesn't it—riding the rails? But it ain't. I took the train the hard way. I waited hidden near the train depot until a freight train started pulling out of the station. Then I slipped aboard one of the cars and rode the train as far as it was going.

The last train I was on dumped me just east of the Cascade Mountains. The only freight I could find heading west that night had cars that were open to the sky—the beautiful sky, with its icy stars twinkling in the frigid air. The weatherman was predicting zero-degree weather in the Cascades that night. That's mighty cold. But it seemed to me that I had only two choices—to freeze to death beside the road, or to freeze to death on an open freight car on a train headed west. I opted for the train.

That option didn't work out so well. I hadn't eaten a thing for days, and my senses were numb with hunger and fatigue.

And the dad-blame air was even colder than I thought. The wind blew around the freight car, whipping into the wide-open doors and right through my worn-out old coat as I thumped and thudded against the boards of the car. I kept slipping into a kind of dazed doze and then jerking awake, afraid that if I fell asleep, I'd die.

We'd almost reach Leavenworth when I saw a light glowing on the side of the tracks. It was the bright, cheerful light of a campfire surrounded by tents. By jingo, it was a work camp! I was saved. Work camps often welcomed rail-riders like me, and I was sure they'd feed me and give me a warm place to sleep. I let my body go limp and sort of rolled off the car and into the deep snowbank beside the tracks.

I struggled to my feet, the breath knocked clean out of me. The snow was deep, and I had trouble walking the few yards into the camp. My stomach twisted in pain at the thought of food, and I fixed my eyes on the largest tent and plunged forward, trying to call out a greeting to the members of the camp. My whole body was shaking with hunger and fatigue, and the world went dark long before I reached the tent.

When I awoke, my body was lying on a comfortable cot underneath a warm wool blanket. Heaven. I opened my eyes and blinked blurrily at the figure standing at the foot of the bed. "Thank you," I croaked. I thought I saw the man nod to me before my eyelids drooped as sleep tried to reclaim me. I struggled against it, wanting to stay awake. Wanting to know more about my rescuer. I forced my eyes open again and saw the man still standing at the foot of my bed, staring at me. "Who are you?" I whispered, my voice sounding harsh in the silence. "I am your brother," said the figure. It was a strange

19

I AM YOUR BROTHER

response, but I was in no condition to question him further. I went back to sleep.

When I awoke for the second time, I felt refreshed. And very hungry. The reason for my growling stomach made its way through my nostrils and brought me upright almost at once. Someone was making bacon and eggs. I hoped they were for me!

Almost as soon as I sat up, the man was beside me with a plate heaped with food—bacon, eggs, potatoes. There was even buttered toast. I fell to without a word, gobbling down the food as quickly as I could swallow. It was the most nourishment I'd had in weeks. It was only when I'd sopped up the last of the eggs with my toast and practically licked the fork clean that I took another look at my rescuer. He was a tall, thin man with ordinary features. Not a fellow you'd look twice at in the street. But he'd save me, and that was all that mattered.

"Thank you," I said simply. And then I repeated my question from the previous night: "Who are you?"

"I am your brother," the man said. He took the plate from my hands and turned away.

I got up off the cot, straightened up as best I could, and then told the silent figure that I would head to Leavenworth to see if I could catch another train.

"I appreciate your kindness," I said awkwardly. "If I can ever repay the favor . . . " I let the words trail off. In reply, the thin man said for the third time: "I am your brother."

I nodded a few times, not knowing what else to say. Then I headed out of the work camp and down the tracks to Leavenworth. It didn't take me long to locate a few of my fellow rail-riders skulking near the depot. Refreshed in body and spirit, I told them about my experience. And those fellows stared at me as if I'd grown a second head.

"You're crazy," they told me. "That work camp was abandoned years ago. And that fellow you described—old Joe— he's been dead just as long. You must have been dreaming."

I knew I hadn't been dreaming. My stomach was full and I was warm, and those things couldn't be if I'd spent the night in a snowdrift. I bade my companions farewell and stood for awhile, waiting for the train to Seattle. But I couldn't settle down. I kept remembering the strange words of the man at the work camp, and the mocking laughter of my fellow rail-riders.

Finally, I could stand it no longer. I had to go back and look. I slipped back onto the train tracks and walked eastward, away from town. In about half an hour, I reached the place where I'd spent the night, and stood stock-still in amazement. The place was a disaster. Literally, a disaster. No one looked to have lived in or maintained the buildings and tents for years. They were worn out, torn down, decayed beyond repair. And yet, it was the very same place I'd been succored last night by a strange, thin man who could say only one phrase: "I am your brother."

Rubbing my eyes didn't change the scene. I could even see the churned-up snow where I'd fallen from the moving train, and a few rough footprints where I'd staggered toward the work camp. And that was all.

I didn't know if I'd stepped back in time, or if the work camp had been reconstructed for a few hours just for me. All I knew, in that moment of revelation, was that my life had been saved by a ghost.

Mind reeling, I turned slowly away and headed back toward Leavenworth, thinking: "My life must be worth something, if a ghost would come back from the dead to save it." I felt my heart swell with hope. Better days were coming—I knew it. I set my face toward the west, and in a few hours I was on the next freight train, heading to Seattle . . . and my future.

5

The Final Ride

KENT

I was driving my elderly aunt home from an ancient cousin's funeral one rainy afternoon in mid-May, and we got to talking about the afterlife, not an unusual topic on such an occasion. It helped pass the time, especially since the rain was hammering down so hard that I had to slow the car down to a crawl. The car in front of us was obscured by a gray mist mostly consisting of the spray from its own tires, and I could barely make out its red taillights.

"I don't reckon old Ephraim is keen on meeting his Maker," cackled old Auntie Matilda, slapping the armrest on the door for emphasis. "Not that crazy old miser. He wore his poor old wife into an early grave, and he drove away his only son and cheated just about every man who did business with him. Skinflint."

"I really didn't know him," I said absently, slowing even more to make a turn. "Although, come to think of it, the reason I didn't know him was because he cheated my father over a business matter of some sort. I never heard the details."

"That sounds like old Ephraim," said Auntie Matilda in her cracked old-lady voice. "Nasty piece of work, God rest his soul. If the good Lord can find it, that is!"

Ahead of us in the fog, I became aware of a flashing light. An ambulance? A police car? I slowed even further, peering through the rain-washed windshield that my wipers could barely keep clear. Then I realized it was the flashing lights of a train signal.

I brought the car to a stop a few yards from the candy-cane-striped arms that warned cars to go no further. I sighed. I hated waiting for trains.

"I didn't think there was a train scheduled for this time of day," Auntie Matilda said, glaring at the blinking lights through the rain as if they were a personal insult. Auntie Matilda had lived near the train tracks all her life, and she knew the schedule better than the railroad by this time.

"That's odd," I remarked casually, not paying much attention to her comment.

Now that we weren't moving anymore, the mist kicked up by the tires had cleared a bit, and we could see the train tracks clearly. Auntie Matilda's eyes narrowed as she stared at the rain-darkened tracks. "I wonder . . . " she murmured to herself.

I waited for her to continue, but she remained silent. I put the car in park and we sat awhile, staring at the empty tracks as the blinking lights made a pretty pattern on the dashboard and rain rattled down on the roof. We were the only vehicle on that particular road, and no other arrived as we waited and then waited some more for the train.

I glanced both ways down the track and saw no headlamp burning in the distance.

"This is ridiculous," I said after waiting another five minutes. "I'm going to cross."

I reached forward to put the car in gear. Instantly, Auntie Matilda held up a hand to stop me.

"Wait, Rachel," she said. "I'm remembering an old story I heard about this particular crossing."

I took my hand off the gear shift lever and looked at her.

"What story?" I asked, watching the shadows on her face shifting in the blinking lights.

"They say in the old days there used to be a station here—a special station that could be seen only by folks who had the spirit sight. The only train that used the station was a phantom train that came once a decade to collect the spirits of all the criminals and evildoers who had died nearby and take them to their final judgment."

I snorted indelicately and said: "Auntie Matilda, that's ridic . . . "

I didn't finish my statement. I couldn't, because at that moment, a huge old-fashioned steam train appeared out of nowhere . . . I mean nowhere . . . and chugged along past the blinking warning lights and the flimsy guardrail. Like all old steam engines, it howled and roared and chugged and sighed deeply as it pulled up in front of us. Just off to my left, a bustling depot full of translucent figures had appeared.

The depot was not quite in the same plane as we were. It was angled about 40 degrees up from level ground, and the folks queuing up were sort of hanging in the air as the train drew up to the platform. It was amazing. It was terrifying.

My teeth started to chatter as I watched the old steam train with its many, many cars halt before the station. It was strange, because the milling people and the steaming train were so clear, and yet I could see the road right through them.

My gaze went to the faces of the people who were boarding the train, and chills ran over my skin. All of them, men and women both, had hard, desperate eyes, and cruel, twisted mouths. They were the kind of people you see in your nightmares.

Suddenly, Auntie Matilda grabbed my arm and pointed. "Look, Rachel. Look!"

I followed her hand and saw my cousin Ephraim boarding the passenger car right in front of us.

"That old rapscallion! Serves him right for the way he treated his wife," Auntie Matilda said. Her words were harsh, but her voice trembled, and so did her hand on my arm.

Above us, there came a sudden clap of thunder, and the rain became a torrential downpour. Through the sheets of water, I saw the train start up again and slowly continue on its way. But the track it followed led down and down. A moment later, it vanished from sight. And at the same time, the flashing railway lights blinked out, and the gate began to rise.

We sat in complete silence as the rain pounded the car. I was shaking all over, and my stomach felt strange. I couldn't believe what I'd just seen. Had it been real? I'd have thought I'd imagined it—except that Auntie Matilda had seen it too.

I think I would have sat there forever if a car hadn't suddenly pulled up behind us and beeped its horn. With trembling hands, I put the car in gear and eased over the tracks. Then I carefully drove through the downpour until I reached Auntie Matilda's house near the train station. The real train station.

I grabbed my umbrella and ran around the car to help her out. As I walked her to the porch, she took my hand and pulled me to a stop.

"Now, don't you go a-worrying about that phantom train, Rachel," she said, looking up into my pale face with her dark,

THE FINAL RIDE

snapping eyes. "Only them that deserves it board that train, like your cousin Ephraim. Folks like us, we go on a different train. A heavenly one. And don't you forget it."

I drew in a deep breath. Let it out. Took another one. Then said: "Yes, Auntie Matilda."

She gave me a comforting hug then hobbled up the steps to her front door and disappeared inside.

Inside. Yes. That was a good idea. Suddenly, all I wanted was to get inside my house, have a cup of tea, and forget all about the phantom train that had come for my cousin Ephraim. I furled my umbrella, bolted into my car, and drove home. By the time I got there, I'd half-convinced myself that what I'd seen was a figment of my imagination. Some weird kind of mist that came with the rainstorm. And I almost believed it.

But I have to admit, I've never driven down that particular road again since that day. Just in case.

6

The Extra Student

She laughed to herself when she woke in darkness in the wee hours of the morning. It never failed. No matter how many years she had been teaching, she still got excited and nervous on the first day of a new term. She tried to get back to sleep, but her mind was racing through her lesson plans, and she kept wondering what her new students would be like. An hour before her alarm rang, she finally gave up trying to sleep.

She was in the classroom early, tidying her things. She spent half an hour putting together a welcome bulletin board and swept the floor so thoroughly that folks could probably eat off it. Eventually, she heard voices in the hallway as the other teachers slowly trickled into the academy. When she poked her head into the teachers' lounge, she was greeted with friendly waves and happy voices teasing her about her preterm nerves. She relaxed and went to join her colleagues, happy to be back.

Finally—finally—the first bell rang, and her first class came rushing in. They were eager and lively and full of high spirits. She felt her heart lift at the sight of their fresh faces, and soon a lively dialogue between teacher and new students was established. They liked her, she could tell. And they were smart, too. She tossed review questions at them to see how much information they'd retained from the previous grade, and they were quick to answer. And most of the answers were correct.

One little lad, sitting in one of the front desks, was particularly knowledgeable. She was impressed by his answers, and more impressed by the fact that he didn't push himself forward as the class "know-it-all." He answered quickly and quietly and let others take their turns. He had bright blue eyes and curly dark hair, and his smile was impish. He seemed to soak in information like a sponge. The teacher smiled back at him and tossed out another history question, seemingly at random, which he answered promptly after a pause indicated that no one else knew the answer.

At that moment, the bell rang. The teacher sighed and then smiled. Her first class of the term had been a success. To her surprise, the curly-haired boy in the front row jumped up from his seat and hurried toward the door without waiting for her to dismiss the class. That seemed strange, after his polite behavior during class. She opened her mouth to reprimand him and then gasped as he walked straight through the wall beside the closed door and vanished.

The teacher's eyes widened, and her mouth went dry. Around her, the students exclaimed in shock and fear.

"Did you see?" shrieked one of the girls. "Did you see? He went right through the wall!"

"A ghost! He was a ghost," another boy shouted.

Pandemonium reigned as students from the first class shrieked and chattered, and students filing in for the next class tried to figure out what was going on. The teacher sat on the edge of her desk feeling faint and dizzy. It wasn't until a student

THE EXTRA STUDENT

brought her a drink of water that she recovered herself enough to dismiss the first class and welcome the second.

Over lunch, the teacher told the story to her colleagues in the teachers' lounge. Those who had been at the academy the longest exchanged knowing glances. In hushed voices, they told her that the school had the reputation for being haunted by the ghosts of students who had died too young. Footsteps were heard after hours. Janitors reported the sounds of children talking and laughing inside darkened classrooms, and sometimes the teachers themselves had felt invisible presences rushing down the empty hallways.

"They don't like us to talk about it," the math teacher added. "I think you're the first teacher to actually see a ghost student in the classroom. But we've all felt them."

The others nodded solemnly, and the teacher felt goose bumps rise on her skin. Ghosts in the building. In her classroom. She didn't like the thought. Not at all.

The teacher gathered up her purse and her bags at the end of the day in a thoughtful mood. It had been an interesting day, full of all sorts of students: eager, belligerent, tired, happy, sad. Oh—and one ghostly!

"They said teaching would be a challenge," she murmured to herself as she left the classroom. "Boy, they weren't kidding."

She paused for a moment and glanced back at the desk where the ghost student had sat. Everyone had refused to sit there that day, even the students who hadn't seen the ghost. And she didn't blame them. A shiver ran through her body. Should she keep teaching at a haunted school? Then she remembered the ghost boy's happy grin, and her fear faded. Maybe she should. She waved a hand at the empty desk and headed home to dinner.

7

The Last Vigilante

ROCKFORD

They were all intoxicated that night. A little too intoxicated, as it turned out. Which was why, an hour or so after hearing the drunken ramblings of the town ne'er-do-well, the seven of them were standing under this tree, staring at the cooling body of young farmer Neil, whom the self-appointed vigilantes had just strung up as a horse thief.

Fred had been shaken by the vehemence of the young farmer's denial of the crime. The more so because, upon reflection, he'd had only the word of the town drunk that Neil was responsible for the thefts. But what was worse, he thought, stumbling backward to get away from the horrible dead face and lolling tongue, was the feeling that they had just murdered an innocent man. Judging from the looks on the faces of his fellow vigilantes, he was not the only one to have second thoughts, now that it was too late.

Then too, there was the curse. As they rode back to town, leaving the poor hanging farmer for his missus to find, Fred recalled the words the young farmer had screamed: "You'll wish you'd shared this tree with me! You—all of you—will die screaming!"

THE LAST VIGILANTE

By consensus, the vigilantes headed back to the bar where they'd started the night's evil work. Fred glanced over at his brother—one of their band—and tried to catch his eye. But his brother avoided his gaze and quickly drank down his whisky. It was clear that the seven vigilantes were feeling guilty. Finally, their leader put his tankard on the bar with trembling hands and whispered: "My God. What have we done?"

They were soon to find out.

The West was wild in those days, and no sheriff came forward to arrest them. But a few days after the killing of young farmer Neil, the leader of the group—old Abe—went missing. Folks turned out to look for him, but it took days for them to locate his body. Where or how he died was a mystery, but his half-eaten corpse was eventually found in the pigsty on the Widow Neil's farm, near the tree where the vigilantes had hung her husband. The twisted look of fear on the corpse's face suggested that this vigilante had—true to the prediction of the curse—died screaming.

Fred went out and got drunk after attending the funeral. He had to. It was that or risk again seeing the farmer's twisted face hovering over his friend's casket, wrapped in flames and grinning wickedly. Fred wondered why none of his fellow vigilantes had commented upon the apparition. They must have seen it. But no one said a word, so he too kept silent.

Silence was much harder to bear when he heard about Wes, the second of the vigilantes to die. Wes was a miller, and he was guiding a skid of logs into his mill when the brand-new chain suddenly burst, and Wes was crushed to death by the falling logs. He died screaming as his body was pummeled and then crushed. Fred nervously asked the other workers at the mill if they'd seen anything before the accident. They shook their heads, mystified. One fellow volunteered that he'd caught a funny whiff of burning, like the hot fire you smelled in a blacksmith's shop, a few moments before the skid tore lose. Fred shuddered and turned away quickly before the worker saw the look on his face. In his mind, he pictured the dead face of farmer Neil as he had seen it at Abe's funeral—tongue lolling, face twisted with flames. Now two of the vigilante band were dead. Two.

He'd barely reached home after talking with the men at the sawmill when he saw a weeping woman standing on his brother's porch across the road. She was speaking to his sister-in-law and wringing her hands. Fred recognized her at once. She was the wife of Nate, another of the vigilantes that had hanged farmer Neil.

His heart sinking, Fred hurried over and learned that Nate had been trampled to death by his team of horses. They were usually placid, but they had spooked suddenly that afternoon.

"As if they'd seen a ghost," Nate's wife moaned through her tears. "Nate started screaming about fire and brimstone just as the horses' hooves caught him."

She collapsed, weeping, and Fred left her to the ministrations of his sister-in-law and fled to his home, stomach roiling. Three dead. Three! And they all died screaming, just as young farmer Neil had said.

The remaining vigilantes gathered at the tavern that night, not saying much. But they kept glancing darkly at Sam, the drunk who'd gotten them into this mess with his false stories about a horse thief. They all reminded each other to take care as they parted for home, though they didn't say aloud what they had to watch out for. Better not to disturb the farmer's dead spirit by speaking about the curse.

And they did take care. Several days passed without incident. No ghostly face appeared before Fred's eyes as he went about his daily work, and he took this as a hopeful sign. Until the report came about Ben, his friend and fellow vigilante. Afraid of the dead farmer's curse, Ben had carefully waited for a windless day to repair his very tall windmill. Once he was sure that the day would remain calm, Ben had climbed to the top of the windmill to oil the blades. Suddenly—out of a clear blue sky—a huge gust had shaken the windmill and thrown a screaming Ben sixty feet down onto the rock-hard ground. The doctor who wrote the death certificate said that every bone in his body had been broken and that his neck was snapped as sharply as if he'd been hanged.

The three remaining vigilantes were now in a panic. Fred jumped whenever anyone spoke to him, and he trembled all the time. His brother was in no better shape. And as for Fritz—well, he woke in the middle of the night after reading about Ben's death, and in his agitation knocked over a lantern and set himself and his house ablaze. The neighbors heard him screaming but couldn't reach him through the flames. When his burnt body was removed from the ashes, his hands were gripped around his throat as if he had been choking when he died.

Fred locked himself into his house when he heard about Fritz's death and refused to come out. And his brother . . . well, he put a gun to his head and shot himself. Only his hands were shaking so hard that the bullet went amiss. So his brother died slowly, in screaming agony, and no one could help him.

Upon hearing the report of his brother's death, Fred ran into town and flung himself into the sheriff's office, babbling about curses and fire and brimstone. All Fred could see, everywhere he looked, was young farmer Neil's face, circled in flames, his tongue lolling grotesquely from his mouth. Every moment, the face grew more withered, writhing with maggots and with sharp bones tearing through rotting flesh.

Deciding that Fred was mad, the sheriff had him committed to a local asylum, where he died a few weeks later, screaming of fire and brimstone and young farmer Neil.

The story of farmer Neil's curse and the death of the vigilantes was repeated so often that it became part of local legend. A few years after the death of the last vigilante, a reporter heard the story of the curse and went to investigate. He searched for and found the old Neil place, but he couldn't find the fabled hanging tree. When he questioned the locals, the reporter learned that the hanging tree had been blasted into smithereens when it was struck by lightning not long after the death of Fred, the last vigilante. And killed by the same blast was old Sam, the drunk who had set the vigilantes after an innocent man. The spirit of farmer Neil was appeased at last.

8

The Rocking Chair

When I saw two old-fashioned his-and-her antique cherry rocking chairs through the window of the antiques store, I knew that they would look perfect in the living room next to the pot-bellied woodstove I recently had installed. The lady's rocking chair had a tapestry cushion, and the man's had a dark leather seat. The woman in the shop said they were made in the empire style around 1880. When I sat in the lady's rocker, it fitted my kinks perfectly. The man's rocker was also sinfully comfortable, and I took them home at once—well wrapped—in the back of my SUV.

The rocking chairs gave my living room a lovely, homey air. I placed one on either side of the stove, facing the TV, and laid my grandmother's quilt over the back of the lady's rocker. I put the old end table I'd inherited from my grandparents next to the man's rocker. It seemed appropriate. My grandfather had used the drawer in the end table for his pipe and smoking paraphernalia. *He would have liked the man's rocker,* I thought with a pleased smile.

My cat, Mollie, chose that instant to sidle into the living room to inspect the new furniture. She purred and rubbed against the lady's rocker in an approving manner. But when she approached the man's rocker, she arched her back, all her hair standing on end, and hissed. Then she raced out of the room, tail bristling, as if she'd had a fright. I stared after her, puzzled, and then looked back at the rocker. There was nothing there that I could see. I shrugged and went to put another load of clothes in the washing machine.

It was about eight o'clock that evening when I heard the TV rumbling out a commercial in the front room. I frowned. That was weird. I lived alone, and I hadn't turned the TV on when I installed the chairs that afternoon. Hmm. Maybe Mollie had stepped on the remote control. I went into the living room, and yes, the TV was on. There was no sign of Mollie, but that didn't mean anything. I found the remote control on my grandfather's end table and flicked the TV off.

There was a faint smell of smoke in the air, but it was cigarette smoke, not pipe smoke. I frowned. Were the neighbor's teens smoking in my shrubbery? I opened the window and looked out into the thicket of rhododendron bushes, but no one was there. When I closed the window, I noticed the man's rocker was moving slightly, back and forth, back and forth. For some reason, the sight gave me chills. I shivered and hurried out of the living room.

Behind me, the TV flicked on again. I whirled and glared at the screen, then looked around for Mollie, but there was no one in the room except me. And the gently swaying rocking chair. I grabbed the remote from the end table, turned off the TV, and then put the remote into the drawer of the TV stand. Mollie couldn't reach it there, I knew. I wondered where she was hiding and how she'd gotten off the end table without me seeing her.

I headed back toward the kitchen and almost tripped over Mollie, who had just trotted in through the cat door that led to the patio. I stopped and stared at her, my mouth dropping open in shock. If Mollie was outside the whole time, who had turned on the TV? The mystery bothered me the rest of the evening.

When I came down to breakfast the next morning, there was a cereal box on the table with an empty bowl beside it. That frightened me. I knew I had cleared off the table before I went up to bed the previous night. I stared at the bowl, wondering what to do. Should I call the police? At that moment, the refrigerator door opened by itself and a bottle of milk sailed across the room and landed next to the empty bowl. I let out a shriek and raced out of the kitchen. Behind me, I could hear the rattle of the cutlery drawer as it opened and shut. Then I distinctly heard the sound of a man humming to himself as cereal and milk swished into the bowl.

I crouched at the foot of the stairs, wondering what to do. Then I crept back toward the kitchen, holding an umbrella I'd grabbed from the stand in the entranceway. It was a paltry sort of weapon against a ghost, but I didn't know what else to grab. And I wasn't going into the kitchen unarmed.

I slid cautiously through the doorway into the sunny kitchen and glared at the table. A spoon full of cereal was rising through the air. The bowl of the spoon vanished for a moment into an invisible mouth and then appeared again. I had never heard of ghosts eating, but who knows? This one obviously was. Only the level of the cereal in the bowl was not getting any lower. Weird.

Defiantly, I stepped into the kitchen, grabbed the cereal and milk, and filled another bowl. Then I sat down opposite whoever-he-was and began eating. Mollie came through the cat door, yowled at the sight—or nonsight—of the ghost, and ran back out onto the patio.

The spoon opposite me clattered into the bowl with a satisfied sigh, and I heard footsteps heading down the hall toward the living room. Hastily, I wiped my mouth and followed them, in time to see the man's rocker start to move and the TV controller, once again on the end table, rise up into the air and flick on the TV.

OK, I was seriously freaked. I hastened back to the kitchen. Yes, there was still a full bowl of cereal on the table with a wet spoon in it. Obviously, the ghost thought he could eat, but really couldn't. I sat down, staring at the full bowl and clutching my hair in both hands. What was I going to do? I didn't want to live with a ghost. And where had it come from? The only new things in the house were the two rocking chairs.

It had to be the man's rocking chair. It had to be. The humming had been a man's voice, and the man's rocking chair was the only one that moved by itself. And the controller was beside the chair. For a moment, I wondered if it was my grandfather, come back to watch over me. But I dismissed the idea. I had smelled cigarette smoke in the front room, and Granddad had only smoked a pipe. Besides, Granddad's end table had been in the house for years. If his spirit was attached to it, he would have shown up before now.

I left cat food out for Mollie and went thoughtfully to work. How did one go about checking up on a ghost? Obviously, someone who had not been there before I purchased the rocking chairs was now sharing the house with me. But did ghosts really attach themselves to furniture? I had to find out.

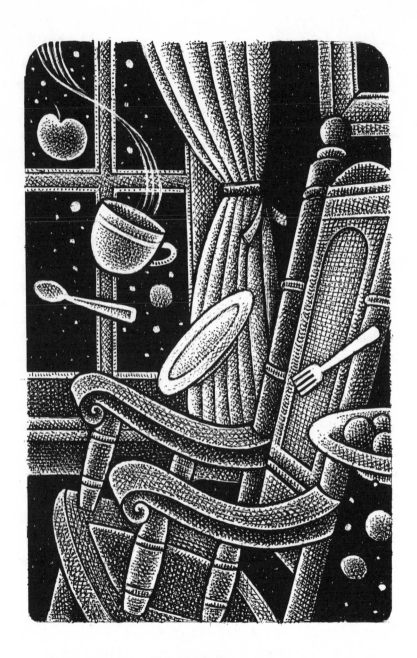

THE ROCKING CHAIR

I spent my lunch hour on the Internet, looking up ghosts and furniture. Sure enough, I wasn't the only one unlucky enough to have purchased a ghost. There were plenty of others who'd bought haunted dressers, trunks, jewelry, and, in one case, a front door, and these poor fools had ended up with spirits a-plenty. However, there was a dearth of information on how to get rid of said spirits without also getting rid of the haunted furniture. That wasn't good. It meant I had to choose between a spiritless house or my new rocking chair.

I frowned, pondering my next move. Then I called the antiques dealer to see if I could learn more about the chairs. According to the woman who sold them to me, they'd been in an attic for years after the death of the old man who'd previously owned them. It was his granddaughter who brought the rockers to the antiques store when she'd cleaned out the old family home. And, yes, when pressed, the woman did admit that the old man had been found dead in the man's rocking chair, which was his favorite seat in the old house.

So now I knew who my ghost was. But how to get rid of him? I flipped through my card file and pulled out the number of a friend who was a psychic. I invited her over to dinner, neglecting to mention the haunted chair. She was always boasting that she could see and hear ghosts. I wanted to see her in action.

Jill arrived promptly at six thirty. As soon as she stepped through the front door, she said: "Do you know you have a ghost in here?"

A chilly wind whipped out of the living room as she spoke, and we both heard a man whistling as his footsteps headed toward the kitchen.

"Do tell," I said sarcastically. We heard Mollie yowl and the invisible man swear.

"He came here with a chair. Does that make sense?" asked Jill, closing her eyes briefly as she concentrated. I pointed into the living room, and Jill looked in at the two new chairs.

"That one," said Jill at once, pointing to the man's rocker.

"So how do I get rid of him?" I asked quietly, conscious of the man humming in the kitchen. A moment later, a plate full of cookies and a glass of milk floated down the hall, swerved around Jill and me, and landed on the end table by the man's rocking chair. The TV flicked on.

Jill was staring at a floating cookie that somehow had not really moved from the plate, and then at the levitating glass of milk—the level of which didn't get any lower, even when it tilted to accommodate an invisible mouth. Impatiently, I beckoned her to the kitchen.

"I am not sharing my home with that man," I said, as I set a steaming plate of spaghetti before my guest. "He's not-really eating me out of house and home! I can't afford all his wasted food, and there's no way I am going to eat any of that stuff after he's not-really touched it!" I added, forestalling Jill's next remark.

"No, I don't blame you," Jill said as I sank down opposite her with my own plate of spaghetti.

"Can you ask him to leave?" I asked, twirling spaghetti around my fork.

"I can try. But from what I'm sensing, I'd say he's a stubborn old fellow and probably won't leave without his chair."

"I paid eight hundred dollars for that chair," I wailed.

"So get your money back from the dealer. Or sell it to somebody else."

"How can I sell a haunted piece of furniture to somebody else?" I asked. "That's totally unethical."

"The store sold it to you," Jill pointed out. "Who knows, maybe it increases the value of the piece, having a ghost attached to it. Some people might pay big money for a specter."

At that moment, there came a crash and a curse from the front room. I raced into the hallway in time to see Mollie flying through the air as if she'd been chucked out of the living room door. Miraculously, she landed on all fours and zoomed up the staircase to the second floor.

"That does it!" I said, furious. I marched into the front room, grabbed the man's rocker, and stalked into the hallway. "Get the door," I shouted to Jill, who got the door without argument. I thrust the chair unceremoniously into the back of the SUV, locked the vehicle, and went back into the house to finish my spaghetti. In the living room, Jill and I both heard a sad sigh as the TV flickered off. Then the sound of footsteps walking through the entryway and out the front door.

"Good riddance," I sniffed.

Jill began to giggle. I glared at her until she explained: "That's exactly what he said as he walked out of the house." I continued to glare at her. "He thinks you're just as hard to live with as his ex-wife," Jill remarked and busted up laughing.

That was so not funny.

After dinner, Jill and I drove to the antiques store, which was open late. I told the dealer about the ghost and demanded my money back. The saleswoman's eyes got wide as she stared from me to the rocking chair, but she reimbursed me with no argument.

"She probably thinks I'm insane," I said to Jill as we left the store.

"Well, you're not. She'll find out the hard way the next time she leaves out her lunch," Jill said.

I sighed as I got back in the SUV. "I really liked that chair," I said.

"You've still got the other one," Jill pointed out cheerfully.

Yes, that was true.

"And Mollie will be happy," she added as I turned the key in the ignition.

True too.

"Besides, he was almost-eating you out of house and home," she reminded me.

That cheered me up. "Very true," I said. "I really couldn't afford the cost of upkeep for that chair anyway."

"These things always work out for the best," Jill said, hiding a grin.

I gave her a sarcastic look and then laughed. I guess they always do.

Sailor's Revenge

PORT TOWNSEND

Billy Murphy was a round, stout little man with chubby red cheeks like a cherub and a perpetually surprised expression. He was so clean-cut and jolly looking that a mother would hand him her baby to mind without a second's thought. Yet in truth, he was one of the most notorious crimpers in town.

Billy had a deal going with the owners of a couple of the local taverns. He'd strike up an acquaintance with any likely looking young men that stopped in Port Townsend—lumberjacks just in from the backwoods, newly employed waterfront workers, army deserters—and offer to buy them a couple of drinks at the tavern. Then he'd slip them a mickey in their beer. When the victim had dropped off, Billy and the bartender would open a secret door in the floor, which was built on top of a pier, and drop the body into a rowboat bobbing below. After they'd trapped the agreed-upon number of young men, they'd row the boat over to the waiting ship and dump the bodies aboard. The captains paid $50 a head for kidnapped crew members.

While Billy and the bartender rowed back to town, the unconscious men were dragged below deck and locked in the hold until the ship was far out to sea. When the poor young fellows woke up with a splitting headache the next morning, they'd find themselves signed aboard a ship bound for Shanghai or other foreign parts, and forced to work as sailors for the duration of the trip.

Billy made quite a good living from his shenanigans—enough to buy him a big house on the hill and win him a pretty wife to fill the house with pretty things. He showed not a whit of remorse for his dishonest dealings, though he was careful to keep the true source of his wealth from his wife. In fact, he considered himself to be doing a public service for the town, cleaning out all the lowlifes who haunted the streets.

Well, they say justice comes to every man, and it finally came to Billy Murphy. One late afternoon, he bumped into a tall, skinny, freckled-face, red-haired boy eagerly roaming the docks. Billy'd never seen the lad before, and he watched him for awhile. He seemed to be alone, and he looked sturdy enough to help crew a ship. Pickings had been slim that day, and Billy still needed one more man to fill the crew-compliment of the three-masted bark out in the bay that needed sailors. So Billy Murphy strolled over and struck up a conversation with the boy.

The lad was pleased by the attention. He chatted happily about the university he was attending, about his family "back East," and about how excited he was to be visiting the Northwest at last. Billy let him talk on and on, and when he volunteered to buy the boy a drink, the lad accepted gratefully. They stopped at Billy's favorite watering hole, and a few drinks later, the boy's body was being dropped on top of a pile of newly recruited sailors that lined the hidden rowboat below the pier. A few hours later, the lad was on his way to Australia, and Billy was $50 richer—minus the bartender's cut.

Billy was feeling smug and self-satisfied when he made his way up the hill for a late dinner with his pretty wife. To his surprise, he found her pacing back and forth in the parlor in agitation.

"Oh, Billy, I'm so glad you're home," little Annabelle Murphy cried when he entered the room. "My cousin Ned Tucker from New York arrived this morning, just after you'd left. Remember I told you he was touring the West Coast during the summer holidays? Well, he went for a walk this afternoon, and he still hasn't come back. I'm quite worried about him. He said he might visit the docks, and there are some rough types down there. Would you be a dear and go look for him?"

Billy's chubby cheeks went white. "What does he look like?" he asked hoarsely. To his horror, Annabelle described in detail the tall, skinny, red-haired boy he'd just dumped aboard the bark heading to Australia. "I'll see if I can find him," Billy told his wife, and raced out of the house as fast as his feet could take him. Perhaps the bark hadn't left. Perhaps . . .

But it was too late. The bark was gone, taking Annabelle's cousin with it. Billy went home with a sinking heart to report the boy still missing.

It took a lot of fancy footwork on Billy's part to keep Annabelle in ignorance of his part in the kidnapping. Annabelle was in quite a state when she was told that the boy had probably been shanghaied. She lay prostrate in bed for three days and wept copiously when she wrote to the boy's parents in New York. It took several months for her to calm down and accept the loss of her young cousin.

"At least he's still alive," Billy told her over and over. "And he will come home with the ship."

But his words did little to comfort Annabelle, and he took care to burn the angry letter that came from her New York cousins without showing it to her.

Billy lost heart for his crimping after that day. Sometimes a week would go by without him luring a single fellow into the tavern, and the bartender started complaining and threatened to turn him in to the authorities if he didn't keep up his end of the bargain. Billy felt trapped between his wife and his career, and he didn't like the feeling. But there really was nothing he could do without moving himself and Annabelle far away from Port Townsend. So he reluctantly carried on crimping.

One evening, about three months later, Billy looked up from a card game in the tavern and gasped in heart-thumping horror. A bloated white face half covered by a shock of red hair was floating near the roof. Seaweed was tangled around its ears and neck, and the blue eyes bulged sightlessly, but Billy could still recognize it as the drowned face of Ned Tucker.

Billy shrieked and leapt up, overturning his beer. Everyone shouted and cursed and looked around for the cause of Billy's fright, but the floating head had disappeared the instant Billy screamed.

Flustered, Billy folded his cards and left the bar. He made his way up the darkened hillside, his body shaking. What had he seen? Was it a vision brought on by too much beer? Or was it something more?

When he got home, he fumbled with the key to the front door, pulling it out of his pocket and then dropping it from his trembling hands. He bent to retrieve it, and when he stood up he saw the bloated face of Ned Tucker staring back at him from the little stained-glass window above the knocker. Billy

SAILOR'S REVENGE

staggered backward in terror, shouting so loudly that Annabelle came running. Billy made up a feeble excuse about stepping on the neighbor's cat and tripped over the doorstep as he walked inside. He fell face-first and bumped his head hard against the edge of a table. For a moment he saw stars, and his dazed senses heard—high pitched against Annabelle's worried contralto—the sound of a boy gurgling and gasping as he drew water into his lungs instead of air. Then the boy began to moan, a sound of despair and longing that raised all the hairs on Billy's body and made him clamp his hands over his ears and sit up, blood streaming down his forehead.

Annabelle forced him to lie back down while she tended to the cut. She wanted to send a servant for the doctor, but Billy overruled her. He would be fine after a good night's sleep, he insisted, his eyes traveling frantically from shadow to shadow around the hallway, searching for a bloated white face. But the moaning had ceased, and the face of the drowned Ned Tucker was nowhere to be seen.

Annabelle and the downstairs maid helped Billy up to bed, and he lay among the sheets trembling from head to toe as if suffering from a high fever.

"I don't care what you say, I'm sending for the doctor," Annabelle said. She nodded to the servant, who rushed away on his errand. Then she sat beside her stout, round little husband and stroked his hand, trying to calm him. But Billy could hear the moaning again. It was a faint, horrible sound, just at the edge of hearing. All the terror and fear and loneliness in the world seemed contained in it. It was the desperate longing of a child for its mother; a longing denied all hope. The sound was far away, and at first it was drowned out by the comforting chatter of Annabelle. But it was coming closer. Closer. And now Billy could hear footsteps approaching the bedroom from vast open distances that had nothing to do with space and time. Footsteps and moaning that came from right outside the world, and they were drawing near.

Beneath the sound came the rumble of a carriage pulling up outside.

"That will be the doctor," Annabelle exclaimed. She dropped a kiss on her husband's hand and ran downstairs to greet him.

The footsteps came closer, and now Billy could see a distant horizon superimpose itself on the far wall. Moving toward him from the vast depths of eternity came the spirit of Ned Turner, his drowned figure draped in seaweed. Closer and still closer. His face was shining obscenely, as if a powerful yet unseen sun was focused upon it. And as he stumbled over the last few yards separating him from Billy's bedroom, his moaning was replaced by a terrible gurgling sound like that of a boy trying desperately to breathe and finding his lungs instead filled with water.

A huge wind swept through the bedroom, bringing with it the damp, salty smell of the sea. The tempest swept aside the bed curtains and tore the blankets right off Billy's shaking body. He sat bolt upright, heart thundering against his ribs, as a bloated, red-haired figure stepped down from the vastness of the eternal horizon and into the bedroom. Its blue eyes stared sightlessly at Billy through the long strands of seaweed crossing its body. Billy screamed once, twice. His scream broke off abruptly as cold hands closed over his throat.

Downstairs in the front hall, the doctor and Annabelle looked up in fear. The doctor took the stairs two at a time, with Annabelle and the servants on his heels. They rushed into the bedroom, which smelled strongly of saltwater and was damp and cold, as if it had been drenched by a storm. Seaweed was draped everywhere, wrapping the still figure lying on the bed like a mummy. Only the face of Billy Murphy was visible. His lifeless eyes bulged grotesquely from his shroud, and the part of his mouth that was still visible was twisted in terror. Blood dripped gruesomely from his eye sockets and from the dent in his forehead.

Bending over the body was a white, seaweed-draped apparition. Its feet floated several inches above the floor boards. For a moment, it gloated in triumph over the body in the bed. Then it rose straight up through the bed's canopy, through the ceiling, and vanished.

The sailor's revenge was complete.

10

Steak and Eggs

SPOKANE

It was no fun being broke, the young wife mused, especially at mealtime. She curled down in her seat as her husband negotiated a turn between a taxi and a large truck. They were driving through downtown Spokane on their way to visit family in western Washington. They were hours from their destination and were hungry and tired and needed a break. Unfortunately, they were also out of money.

"We can't be entirely broke," she said once they were safely turned onto the new street. "I'm going to look around and see what I can find."

The young wife went through her purse and the glove compartment, looking for spare change. She hunkered down on the floor and looked under the seats of the car, trying to find enough money to get them some kind of meal.

She'd collected about eight dollars in quarters, dimes, nickels, and a few grubby dollar bills when her husband called her attention to a signpost: STEAK AND EGGS—$3.85. It was attached to a motel–diner combination in downtown Spokane.

Steak and eggs sounded wonderful to the hungry couple, and the price was right. Armed with their change, they parked the car and walked into the old-time diner—the kind of place laughingly called a "greasy spoon." But the food smelled delicious, the place was packed with customers, and the prices on the yellowing menus were just as good as advertised. The couple had steak and eggs on their minds, and that's what they got.

When their plates arrived, the couple saw that the portions were huge. They could have easily shared a plate and still had leftovers! They dug in with the enthusiasm born of true hunger and polished off every morsel. The friendly waitress kept their water glasses filled and checked back with them frequently to make sure they had everything they needed. "We have to give her a good tip," the young wife whispered to her husband after the kindly woman dropped some extra napkins onto their table.

With such good food and excellent service, the young couple found themselves having a wonderful time. All this for eight dollars, more or less!

"We have to come back here the next time we come to Spokane," the young husband said enthusiastically, and his wife agreed.

Finally, full and ready to continue their journey, the young couple signaled for the bill. When it arrived, the total came to $5. The young husband blinked at the low cost and—checking the bill—found the waitress had charged them only 85 cents for the second meal. The husband immediately called the waitress over and showed her the error, happy to pay full price for such excellent service, even if it meant spending their very last dime. The waitress thanked him for showing her the error but explained that the restaurant's policy was to charge customers only what was written on the bill, even if the server made an error.

STEAK AND EGGS

Impressed, the couple paid the low bill and continued on their journey, but not before picking up a brochure for the attached motel. This was a place to recommend to their friends!

And the couple did recommend the diner and motel combination in Spokane. Many times over. Until the day one of their friends who was familiar with the area questioned them closely about their experience. He'd never heard of a motel–diner combination in the area they'd described, nor of a restaurant by that particular name. So the young wife went back through their things and dug out the brochure. Their friend looked it over, confused. Yes, he'd seen the motel before. But, he added, there was no diner attached to it—at least, he'd never seen one there, and he'd passed it multiple times.

Puzzled, the husband called the number on the brochure and asked about the diner. To his amazement, the staff member who answered the phone told him that the restaurant attached to the motel had burned to the ground many years before the couple had visited Spokane.

Apparently, the needy couple had eaten steak and eggs at a phantom restaurant populated by friendly—and generous—ghosts!

11

Has Anyone Seen My Cow?

STEILACOOMB

I'd looked everywhere for that blasted cow. Up and down the moonlit streets, through people's yards, back in the meadows. But I couldn't find her anywhere. I paused under a streetlamp to scratch at the thrice-blasted itch around my neck, moving the strange collar I found there from one side to the other to get at the worst spots. Ouch. Felt like I had a rope-burn there.

At that moment, a fellow in strange clothes came whistling down the street. I stopped scratching and hurried toward him. "Excuse me, sir," I called out. "Have you seen my cow?" The fellow let out a loud yell and ran away as fast as I'd ever seen a bloke run. That puzzled me a might. What the dickens? Anyone would think he'd seen a ghost.

I found an empty patch of lawn and sat down on it to rest and think. If I were a cow, where would I go? My mind was blank. I'd looked all the places I thought she would go, and she hadn't been there. Maybe, if I thought back over the events of the last few days, I'd remember something useful.

I sat with my head in my hands and thought as hard as I could. I hadn't seen that blasted cow since . . . since . . .

Since the day she'd disappeared, of course, back in 1867. She wasn't in her pasture, and she hadn't wandered into the neighbor's yard like she sometimes did. I wandered around town looking for her and popped my head into a couple saloons to ask the fellows drinking there if they'd seen my cow.

Along about the second or third saloon, one of the regulars sang out that he'd seen my cow's head on a pike in front of Andrew Byrd's slaughterhouse. Well, that riled me up. I loved that cow like she was my child, and to hear that a rich fellow like Byrd had stolen and slaughtered her was more than I could bear. I went running down to the millhouse where Byrd worked and confronted him. We had a terrible fight. The blasted fellow claimed he hadn't killed my cow, and he even told me to look through his slaughterhouse if I didn't believe him. Ha! Did he think I was stupid? He'd never let me into his slaughterhouse unless he'd already cleared away the body of my poor heifer. "Look somewhere else for your missing cow," Byrd told me.

At that, I stomped off in a rage. I didn't even check to see if my poor cow's head was still hanging on the pike. I was furious with Byrd and needed time to figure out what to do.

I wandered around town for days, muttering to myself and planning my revenge. My chance came when the rich miller stopped by the post office about three days after my cow disappeared. I jumped out at him with my gun in hand and shot him right in the torso and the leg. He started running, and I chased him down, hoping to get in a third shot. But the blasted folks hanging around the blasted street stopped me.

'Course, I ended up in jail. They didn't seem to care that Byrd had killed my cow—not at all. I fumed about it all night.

HAS ANYONE SEEN MY COW?

I really missed that cow, and Byrd had taken her from me. The next day, I paced up and down, still in a rage. When the sheriff told me that Byrd had died, I didn't really hear him. All I could think about was my poor dead cow.

And then the sheriff told me my cow wasn't dead. The fellow at the saloon had lied to me. I stared at him blankly, not able to take in the information. He'd lied? The fellow at the saloon had lied? My cow wasn't dead?

My face lit up when the news finally penetrated. "She ain't dead?" I exclaimed. "Well, then, I gotta go look fer her! She's missing, you know. You haven't seen my cow, have you?"

The sheriff shook his head. "Did you hear me at all, Bates?" he asked sadly. "I said your cow ain't dead—but Byrd is. You shot him."

I shrugged, still thinking about my cow. As soon as I got out of the dad-blame cell, I had to look for her. She'd been missing for days and maybe she was hungry.

I didn't pay any attention to the sudden thumping on the prison door, or to the sound of sledgehammers and axes being used to pry it open. A group of fellows I vaguely recognized shoved the sheriff to one side, and a couple of the men pulled me out of my cell. Good. I was free to look for my cow. Except the men threw a rope about my neck and marched me to a local barn instead. I was a little confused. A lead rope was a good thing. I needed one for my cow. But I wasn't sure why they'd put it around my neck until . . . until . . .

I leapt up from my seat on the grass in alarm. I had to look for my cow. My cow was missing and I had to find her. I scratched guiltily at my itching neck, and my hand closed around the rope hanging from it. Hanging . . .

In my mind, I saw a picture of my cow, followed by a picture of Byrd's face when I shot him, and finally the shadow of a beam high up in the barn, and a figure—was it me?—being strung up on the beam by the neck.

I let out a shriek of fear . . . and vanished.

12

The Mausoleum

SAN JUAN ISLANDS

I was seriously creeped out. I mean seriously. I had wanted to go to the movies. But no. My lame-brained boyfriend had other ideas. He'd been hearing stories about some old mausoleum back in the woods that was supposed to be haunted, and he wanted to go. So here we were, driving across the island in my boyfriend's beat-up sedan instead of heading into town to eat dinner at the bowling alley and then head to the movies. I don't know why I go along with his crazy notions, I really don't. (Okay, it's because he's cute. So sue me!)

"You know I am totally against this course of action," I said, clinging to the door handle as Tommy took a turn a little too fast.

"Sometimes you sound like a lawyer," Tommy complained with a grin and a sideways glance. (I was studying pre-law at college.) I made a face back at him, and we both settled against the seats, completely at ease with one another. We were best buddies from as far back as I can remember, but the romance thing was still new. I liked it—mostly.

But I didn't like the idea of visiting the mausoleum. Tommy didn't believe in ghosts, which made it sort of strange that he liked visiting haunted spots. But I did believe. Couldn't help it. Folks in my family have always been psychic. They've sensed invisible presences, known things before they happened, had visions that came true. Some have even seen ghosts. A couple of years ago my mother saw the ghost of a woman walk right through the wall when she was staying at an historic hotel in San Francisco. Creepy.

The sun was already low in the sky when we parked the car and took the path up toward the mausoleum. I grabbed my camera and brought it along—more as a shield than from any desire to photograph the mausoleum. Taking pictures might help keep my mind off ghosts. Tommy gave his special evil laugh as we walked past the fenced-in graves of the old cemetery, and I poked him in the back to make him stop.

"Are you scared?" he asked, making his voice sound all spooky.

"Don't mess with me, boy-o!" I said. "If I get too scared, you'll have to carry me back to the car!"

Tommy laughed and grabbed my hand. It was awkward trying to navigate some of the narrower places hand in hand, but I didn't let go. The path eventually led to a gravel road heading up the hill. In places, the gravel was so ground into the dirt that you could barely see it, and the road was liberally strewn with pine needles. It was kind of pleasant walking with my boyfriend in the woods while the sun cast nodding shadows through the leaves of the trees. Peaceful.

We came around a slight bend, and I caught sight of a tall gateway with a metal arch over the top. In graceful letters, the arch said: "Afterglow Vista." I stopped dead in the middle of the roadway, all the little hairs on my arms and shoulders prickling.

"There it is," Tommy said, stopping beside me.

I shivered. The day was still sunny and warm, but chills were running all over my skin. Tommy started walking eagerly toward the mausoleum that loomed atop a small incline behind the arched gateway. I gulped and took a couple of steps backward. Even from here, I could see the round, open building. It had no walls, just Roman pillars set at regular intervals around a cement floor. The pillars were joined at the top by a circular roof that was open to the sky in the center. A stone table surrounded by stone chairs lay at the middle of the open chamber.

I was very conscious of being alone in the woods, far away from the nearest buildings, with a cemetery between me and the car. And was that a whispering sound I heard, murmuring softly below the rustling of the wind in the trees?

"Come on, slowpoke," Tommy called over his shoulder.

I pulled my camera off my shoulder and waved it at him as an excuse for my hesitation. I snapped a couple of photos, which calmed me considerably, and then followed my crazy boyfriend toward the arched entrance. Beyond the gate, I could see steps leading up the mausoleum. Three steps, then a ramp. Then five steps, and another ramp. At the top, seven steps completely circled the airy, open mausoleum, leading visitors up into the pillared room with its stone table and stone chairs. One of the pillars that supported the domeless roof was broken.

It should have looked beautiful. Stripes of sunlight alternated with stripes of shadow on the cement ramps. The sun was a glowing ball outlining the tops of the trees to the west. The air was warm. And I was seriously freaked out. I wanted to run away as fast as my legs would carry me. My stomach was roiling and I felt bile rise in my throat. Get out of here, my nerves screamed, even as my legs carried me onward.

Tommy had stopped to read the sign beside the gate, which explained who was buried in the mausoleum and the symbolism of the three, five, and seven steps.

"This McMillan fellow was a mason," Tommy said as I came up beside him and snapped another photo. "The table and chairs represent unity after death. Family members are buried at the base of each chair."

I shivered again. Was that a faint murmuring I heard coming from the mausoleum?

"What do the steps mean?" I asked to distract myself.

"They represent the three stages of life, the five orders of architecture, and the seven liberal arts," Tommy read. "And it says that the pillars are supposed to be the same size as the pillars of Solomon's temple. The broken one represents the broken column of life. Man dies before his work is completed." He said the last phrase in his spooky voice, and my body started shaking.

"Stop," I gasped. Tommy turned away from the sign to stare at me.

"You're pretty shaken up about this," he said, and took my hand. "Come on, silly. Nothing's going to get you with me around."

I swallowed and followed him through the gate—and into a nightmare. The green-golden light flickered around us as the leaves tossed gently in the wind. The birds called softly. The stone steps led upward. And I was cold. So cold. I climbed the three steps and walked up the short ramp toward the set of five steps. My knees were shaking so badly I could hardly stand. I paused and snapped a photo with my free hand. And that's when I heard the voices. Unmistakably, there were voices coming from the empty table at the center of the mausoleum.

I staggered backward, dropping Tommy's hand. The voices grew louder, and I thought I saw blue lights flickering above each of the chairs. I whirled away from the mausoleum, stomach heaving. I was trespassing on a sacred place. I shouldn't be here.

I ran. Down the ramp, down the three steps, out of the gate, down the road. I don't even remember turning up the small trail that led through the cemetery to the car. I just know I was fighting my way through the bushes and then running past the white fence that surrounded the older stones, and then down toward the parking lot by the field.

It wasn't until I lay panting against the hood of the car that I realized Tommy had followed me.

"What's wrong?" he cried. "Why did you run?" He fell against the hood beside me, staring at me in concern.

"Didn't you see the lights? Hear the voices?" I gasped.

Tommy shook his head. "There weren't any lights or voices," he said.

I closed my eyes. That's right. Tommy was a skeptic.

Keeping my eyes closed so I couldn't see the look on his face, I described what I'd seen and heard. Beside me, I heard Tommy sigh. "I didn't see anything," he said. "But it's obvious you did. I can't say I believe in ghosts, but I do believe in you, and if you said there were voices, there were voices."

I opened my eyes in relief just as Tommy caught me in his arms. He stroked my hair and back until I stopped shivering and then tucked me into the car. "We can still make the movie if we

THE MAUSOLEUM

hurry," he said, closing the door gently and crossing over to the driver's side. I nodded gratefully, still speechless with fear. I did not like the supernatural. Not at all.

The movie helped a lot, and so did a good night's sleep. The next day I was able to laugh about the incident, at least a little bit. And by that evening, I'd almost decided that I'd imagined it. We were playing computer games at Tommy's house that evening, and I suddenly remembered the pictures I'd taken the day before. I pulled the card out of the camera, and Tommy loaded the pictures onto the computer. We sat side by side, watching yesterday unfold before our eyes. We'd spent most of the day picnicking at the whale-watching park before driving to the mausoleum. And yes, there was a photo of the gate reading "Afterglow Vista." And a picture of the mausoleum. Tommy flicked to the next picture, and we both gasped. It was the last picture I'd taken, just before we'd walked up the ramp. In the photo, we could clearly see the table and chairs at the center of the mausoleum. And hovering over each of the chairs was a round, blue light!

Goose bumps prickled over my arms and legs. I grabbed Tommy's hand frantically. So I hadn't imagined it. Beside me, Tommy had gone white.

"Hail Mary, full of grace," he whispered, "the Lord is with thee; blessed art thou among women . . . " He recited the entire prayer without realizing what he was saying, wringing my hand in his lap as he spoke.

"I knew you'd seen something," he said at last. "But I had no idea . . . " His voice trailed off. "Do you want me to delete it?"

I swallowed. Thought about it. Shook my head.

"No. Save it. And take a good look at it the next time you want to visit someplace spooky, okay?"

Tommy swallowed too and then nodded. "That won't be anytime soon," he said, glancing again at the lights hovering over the chairs.

"Good," I said, leaning over to turn off the computer monitor. "Good!"

13

Get Out!

BREMERTON

The old woman had no idea, when they sold her the house, that it was haunted. It didn't come up in any of the Realtor's conversations about the place. But of course, it wouldn't. Why jinx a sale? So the ghost—when it first manifested itself—came as a bit of a shock.

It happened the second night that she stayed in her new house. Just as she was drifting off to sleep, she heard a child's voice say: "Get out of my house!" The words were spoken right in her ear, and she jerked awake, pulse pounding wildly.

She was not a young woman, and she didn't recover quickly from surprises. She lay gasping for a few minutes, trying to convince herself that she'd imagined the whole thing. Then she went downstairs and warmed up some milk to calm herself. Surely it was just a dream? She drank the milk and went back to her bedroom. The air was chillier here, and she walked through a cold spot near the closet that made her wince. But at last she relaxed under the covers and felt sleep settling down around her. Later, she decided she had imagined the horse's whinny she'd heard as she drifted off.

A week later, she was mounting the stairs with a vase of

flowers in her hands when a paper-thin, two-dimensional apparition of a little girl appeared at the top of the steps. She looked more like an upright black-and-white playing card than a person, and she was slightly out of focus.

"Get out of my house!" the apparition cried, shaking arms as thin as paper at her. The old woman dropped the vase, spilling flowers and water all down the staircase.

"L . . . look what you made me do," she scolded the ghost in a high-pitched, trembling voice.

"Get out of my house," the ghost girl repeated. Then she started twirling around in a dizzying circle that got smaller and smaller until she disappeared.

The old woman sat down abruptly on the steps, shaking. There was no doubt in her mind that she'd seen a ghost. But who was she? And why was she so angry? It took nearly ten minutes to calm herself, and another ten to clean up the mess. Really, this came as quite a shock!

About a month later, the old lady opened her front door to find a horse grazing in the yard. It was coal black and beautiful. It was also floating a good foot above the ground. The old lady let out a shriek, leapt back inside the house, and slammed the door. She leaned against it, panting, and distinctly heard the nasty snickering of a cruel child who liked to play practical jokes. "Get out of my house," the girl's voice said from the window overlooking the front yard.

"No," the old lady said in her firmest voice. "You get out."

A snort of rage came from the empty air. And a moment later, the back door slammed expressively.

The old lady turned the handle of the front door, opened it slowly, and peeked outside. The horse was gone.

GET OUT!

"I've had about enough of this," she told herself. Time to find out what was going on. She went to the local newspaper office and went through the archives, searching for information about the death of a little girl and—as an afterthought—a black horse. It took a while for her to locate the story. It had happened nearly fifteen years ago. A little girl and her horse were struck by a drunk driver one evening on their way home. It was dark, and the horse was black, and the driver just didn't see them in time. Animal and child were both killed. The child's home address was the same as the old lady's. So this was her ghost.

The old lady also found a reference, just last year, to the death of first one and then another of the child's parents. Apparently, the house had gone to a distant family member, who had sold it—with its resident ghost—to her.

The old lady sat thoughtfully at the desk after she'd finished her research. The child was probably missing her parents and was angry that a stranger lived in her house. But short of selling the house and moving away, there was nothing the old lady could do. Hopefully, the little ghost would become reconciled to the new owner and would rest in peace at last.

But that was not to be. The appearances of the little apparition became more frequent. The two-dimensional figure would leap out at the old woman from behind doors. She would shout in the old lady's ear while she was holding fragile objects. The horse appeared in the house—chewing on the curtains in the parlor, swishing its tail over the quilt on her bed, crowding into the kitchen with a paper-thin rider on its back.

But the old lady was just as stubborn as the ghost. Whenever the ghost shouted: "Get out of my house," the old lady shouted back: "No!"

One evening in late summer, the old lady entered the kitchen holding a basket of tomatoes, and the ghost attacked her with a knife. The old lady just managed to parry with the basket, and the knife flew out of the ghost's hands and clattered to the floor. Her whole body shaking in terror, the old lady realized the ghost had attacked her with the cleaver she used for cutting meat.

"Get out of my house!" the shimmering, black-and-white, paper-thin ghost screamed at her. Behind her, she felt the cold whoosh of a ghost horse's breath on her neck. "GET OUT!"

The old lady flushed a brilliant red and threw the basket of tomatoes at the shimmering ghost-girl.

"NO!" she screamed. And felt a horrible pain rip through her left arm, fill her chest, smash through her mind. The world turned searing white, and she felt her body tumbling to the floor amidst the rolling red tomatoes.

A visiting neighbor found the body and called the police. The doctor said the woman had died of a massive heart attack, and the matter ended there. None of the visitors to the house heard the rude, high-pitched laughter coming from the front parlor, and the doctor walked right through the body of the coal-black horse grazing in the vegetable garden by the back door.

No one else bought the house after the old lady died. The people who came to view it were frightened off by slamming doors, cool breezes, and a sense of menace. The house fell into disrepair, and the town eventually had it torn down.

But they say that on moonless nights, people driving down the road where the house once stood sometimes see a black horse trotting beside them. On its back is the shimmering, black-and-white figure of a little girl, who waves paper-thin arms and shouts: "Get out!"

PART TWO
Powers of Darkness and Light

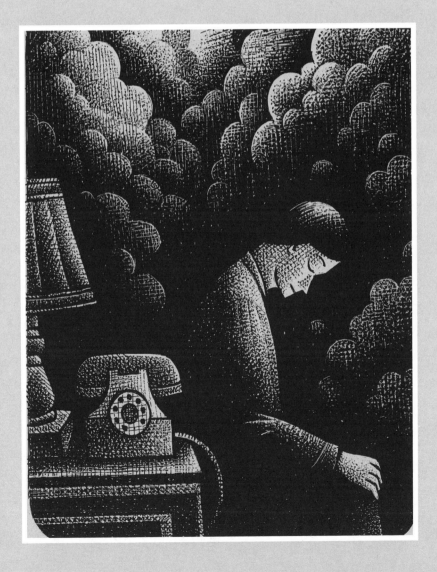

14

Thirteen Steps

MALTBY

It began as a joke. The fellows and I liked to play pranks on people, and the new boy in school was a perfect target. He was small and wiry and wore huge goggle-eyed glasses that made him look like a geek. And that's what he was. A geek who had brains spilling out of his ears. You had to follow him around with a dictionary if you wanted to understand what he was talking about. Most of us didn't bother. School was school—something to be endured, not enjoyed.

We plagued the life out of Brian the geek, playing all the silly jokes that rough-and-tumble jocks usually play on the head of the class. Stole his pants in the locker room so he had to wear gym shorts all day; left him stuck by the seat of his jeans to a hook on the wall of the gymnasium; jammed his locker door shut. You get what I mean.

It was Tommy who suggested we invite Brian to go to the cemetery with us on Halloween night. We always went out on Halloween, looking for a good scare. And we'd heard about a local place that had a spooky underground vault. Folks called its staircase the "Thirteen Steps to Hell," and told all the schoolchildren to avoid it. You know, grown-ups should know better. As soon as we heard the story, we decided it was the perfect place to spend Halloween night.

Brian was thrilled to join the popular boys in their spooky adventure. You'd think he'd have learned by now—with that head full of brains—that we were up to no good. But he came along anyway.

It was cold that night. An extreme, wintery-type cold. The drizzle, as we set out, soon soaked our thick jackets and made the bike ride miserable. It was dark and spooky on the back lanes, and hard to see without streetlights. A couple of fellows had flashlights, so we made do. But the shadowy roadways with the tall trees crowding too close for comfort made my skin crawl. The bare branches reached out toward me like skeletal hands, and I kept imagining that something big and, well, not human was keeping pace with our bikes as we rode down the twisted road toward the cemetery.

I wasn't the only one who was nervous. Several of the fellows were talking too loud and making stupid jokes. And Brian's mouth seemed to be on autopilot. He kept chattering about this and that, using words that would ensure him a place at Harvard University some day if I didn't miss my guess.

Our eyes had adjusted to the darkness by the time we entered the cemetery. It was raining harder now, and there was a white mist swirling around the gravestones. I saw a shape in the darkness—tree or gravestone, I couldn't tell which—that looked like the hooded figure of Death; its arms were open wide, as if to pull me into a dark embrace. I ducked away from the shape, and the wind rose around me, howling like the demons of hell. It slammed the rain into my shivering flesh as I peddled along the lane with the others. An icy, finger-like breeze blew across my neck and tickled my ears, making them tingle. A swirl of mist crossed my vision for a moment, and I swore aloud, seeing grotesque faces in the gray swirls.

"Steady, old man," Tommy said, peddling up beside me. "We're almost there."

"I can't wait to get out of this rain," I grumbled, glaring at the swirling mist and the hulking black gravestones rising from it.

But the creepiness of the graveyard palled as we rode into the shadowy corner where the flat stone marking the underground vault lay. The rectangular stone seemed to be covered in strange patterns that looked like the writing of some black-magic script used to summon demons. The air around the stone was freezing cold. The rain froze in midair a foot above our heads and fell to the ground as ice. Brian exclaimed excitedly over the phenomenon and—good grief, I couldn't believe what I was seeing!—he actually pulled a magnifying glass and a thermometer from the pocket of his jacket to study the strange, icy conditions.

I turned away—and immediately wished I hadn't. The strange script on the stone seemed to be writhing, and very faintly, behind the patter of the rain, I heard sibilant voices hissing in the wind. The wind had a greasy feel, and it crawled along our faces and hands like some evil witch's caress. There were no more jokes now, no loud voices. Every fellow in our little cavalcade was white-faced, wide-eyed, and silent. Finally, Tommy shook himself all over, spattering us with raindrops, and said: "Come on, fellows, let's shift it."

Each of us hesitated—gulping and shivering—then grabbed a corner or side of the heavy stone. It took a lot of panting and shuffling and cursing, but we finally managed to shift it to one side. By that time, the icy air that blasted out of the gaping black hole under the stone felt good on our sweating bodies. And yes, I could just make out a couple of steps leading down into the darkness below.

I hated the sight of those dark steps, and I backed away from the black hole we had uncovered. It looked like the mouth of a monster, waiting for me to step inside so its sharp teeth could shred my skin and gnaw my bones.

Brian came loping up to our little huddle, making some of the fellows jump. "There's a twenty-degree differential between the air by those gravestones and the air here," he announced gleefully as he slipped and slid on the ice by the gaping jaws of the stone tunnel. Just below the sound of his eager voice, I heard the same hissing I'd heard before. This time it came from the tunnel.

"Gruesome thing, isn't it?" Brian said cheerfully, peering down at the gaping hole. I wanted to hit him. How dare he be cheerful in this foul place?

"Come on fellows, let's go to hell," he added, loping into the gaping black maw and out of sight. We heard his feet clattering down the staircase. One step, two, three. Beside me, Tommy straightened his shoulders. There was no way he was going to be outdone by a geek. He marched downward into blackest darkness, and we followed at his heels.

I was the last one to step down onto the staircase. As soon as my foot hit the first step, I was overwhelmed by the sound of screaming. It roared in my ears, wails of agony slicing through my body like knives. I stopped abruptly, my legs shuddering so hard I couldn't walk. I felt cold—bitter cold—but all I could see, dancing on a backdrop of pure darkness, were flames.

THIRTEEN STEPS

Flames sharper, brighter, and more deadly than the roaring, spouting lava of a volcano. Blackened, burning hands stretched forth from the flames, reaching toward me. Reaching . . .

I screamed and stumbled backward, my arms pinwheeling in an effort to keep upright. The howling grew louder, and skeletal, burning figures—some of them horrifyingly familiar—lunged toward me, as if they—like the hooded figure I'd seen in the cemetery—wanted to pull me into their burning embrace. I stumbled over the massive stone that had hidden the staircase and fell into an icy puddle. As soon as I crossed the threshold, the flaming vision ceased as abruptly as it had begun.

The screams did not. But these were human screams now, coming from inside the underground vault, followed by the very real sound of feet pounding up a stone staircase. The fellows burst out of the tunnel, stumbling and cursing as they fell over me. Tommy was the last one out, and over his shoulder he carried the unconscious figure of Brian. Even in the dim light cast by the swirling, icy mist, I could see that Brian's face was twisted into a mask of horror, and blood gushed from his nose and trickled out of his ears.

We ran for our bikes, and Tommy rode double, carrying Brian with him while I pulled Brian's bike along next to mine. We headed straight for the nearest house, and the alarmed family within called instantly for help. According to Tommy, Brian had stopped dead at the bottom of the staircase, his eyes bulging in horror at some sight the others couldn't see. Before they reached the bottom, he gave a small gasp, almost a sigh, and fell to the floor of the tunnel, bleeding profusely from nose and ears. The other fellows had fled at the sight, but Tommy had rushed down the remaining steps to scoop up the injured boy, keeping his eyes firmly fixed on Brian as something bright and menacing twitched at the edges of his sight and a horrible moaning filled his ears.

Brian was rushed to the hospital, and we had to tell our story over and over again to the police before we were sent home in disgrace. I was surprised, frankly, that they believed us. But apparently we were not the only ones to have reported this phenomenon. According to school reports the next day, Brian was in critical condition at the hospital after having taken a "fall down the steps." When he awoke from his coma two days later, he was babbling insanely about flaming figures and the terrors of hell. He made no sense at all, and he was finally sent to a special hospital for the insane. He died there, a year later.

The matter was hushed up, of course. No one wanted a repeat of Brian's experience. NO TRESPASSING signs were posted all over the cemetery, and shortly after Brian's death, a bulldozer dug up the thirteen steps to hell and buried the whole area deep under earth and gravel.

I never told anyone what I'd seen at the top of the thirteen steps that night. Compared to what Brian must have witnessed, it was small stuff. But I never went back to that cemetery. And my parents were amazed at how eager I was thereafter to attend our parish church. From what I'd seen in that graveyard, I wasn't taking any chances on my eternal fate. One glimpse was enough.

15

Tree Octopus

OLYMPIC PENINSULA

When chickens started disappearing from farms and homesteads all over the settlement, folks thought that a family of coons was raiding the local henhouses. But I wasn't so sure. Coons are tough, all right, but usually they leave signs behind: blood, feathers, maybe a few tufts of their own fur, if the rooster put up a fight. And there weren't any of those signs anywhere. These chickens were disappearing into thin air, and the hens around them were giving nary a cluck of warning.

Old Man Hudson sat up in his henhouse one night with his shotgun, looking to kill him a coon. In the morning three chickens were gone, and Hudson none the wiser. He raved about it one night in the tavern over the steady tap-tap-tapping of the rain against the tin roof. He swore up and down that it must be evil spirits getting his chickens. Which was just plain nonsense. It weren't haunts getting the chickens. It was a tree octopus.

Oh, folks may scoff when I talk about tree octopuses, but I knew for a fact they existed. My Granddaddy'd worked for the Hudson Bay Company way back when, and he'd passed down some strange stories about the time he spent hunting on the peninsula. One rainy summer, he was trekking through the deep forest when he came nose to beak with one of them critters. Huge it was, and ugly as all get-out. Granddaddy startled that there octopus as much as it startled him. It rose up tall on all eight of its suckered legs and scurried away through the ferns and up the nearest Douglas fir, quick as you please. Peeked down at Granddaddy with one dark liquid eye from about fifty feet up, and when he saw Granddaddy staring at him, he climbed up even higher, until Granddaddy lost sight of him. Granddaddy was so shocked that he forgot to aim his gun until the critter was gone. He never even took a shot at it.

Granddaddy asked around the settlement about the strange critter he saw in the rainforest, and most folks laughed and called him crazy. But one old coot who'd spent a lot of time in the rainforest pulled him aside and told him it was a rare species of octopus that had adapted to life on land in the rainiest parts of the Northwest. They bred in the Puget Sound, and once the eggs hatched, the baby octopuses came on land and made their way into the rainforest. When they got there, the critters built themselves dens way up in the tallest trees, drinking the rainwater and eating tree frogs and insects and birds and such. They were hard to detect 'cause they could change their color like chameleons, but a good hunter could learn to spot them. The old coot added the rider that Granddaddy'd better be careful, 'cause them tree octopuses could grow quite large. One huge octopus had once run off with the old man's hunting dog while he was busy cooking dinner over the campfire. "Never saw the dad-blame dog again, and he was the best huntin' dog I ever trained," the old man concluded mournfully, pulling out his handkerchief and blowing his nose like a foghorn.

Well, after that conversation, Granddaddy kept his eyes open for tree octopuses whenever he hunted on the peninsula. Saw them a couple more times, but never did shoot one. I think he had a soft spot for the critters. 'Course, folks thought he was telling tall tales, but our family knew better. Granddaddy swore on a stack of Bibles that it was true, and we believed him.

Anyhow, one morning my wife went out to feed the hens after breakfast, and she found six of them gone, just like that. She came running back into the house, fired up with anger. "You better get that coon, Jeremiah Smyth, before it eats all our roasters," she roared at me. "Otherwise, you ain't getting a bite of chicken to eat come wintertime!"

Now, that was a threat to make any mortal man sit up and take notice. No fried chicken or chicken and dumplings this winter? That was downright cruel. I didn't tell my wife she was wrong about a coon getting the chickens. I just said: "Yes, dear" and grabbed my gun. Like I told my boys, the key to a happy marriage is knowing when to shut your trap and do what the little woman wants. And this was one of those times.

Once I got outside, though, I had me a mull over the matter. I knew how to kill a coon. Anyone living in the settlement learned that real quick. Heck, we knew how to bring down much larger game than that. But I never heard anyone talk about how to kill him an octopus. I'd better have a chat with some of the fishermen who caught the danged things in the sea.

Shouldering my rifle, I headed down to the sound to try to catch one of 'em. I had to search awhile before I located a fella who actually fished for octopus. He liked to eat them fried up like chicken. (Sounded awful to me, but it takes all kinds, as my Granddaddy used to say.)

Anyhow, most of the fishermen considered them nuisances 'cause they got caught up in the fish traps along with the fish, but my new pal actually set traps for the dang things. Lowered a baited trap down near their underwater den and pulled 'em up the next day to see if he'd caught anything. Sort of like fishing fer crabs. He asked me why I wanted to know, and I told him about my Granddaddy and the tree octopus. Expected him to laugh at the story, but apparently he'd heard of them from some of the native tribesmen who sometimes hunted them with spears and nets.

After wishing me good hunting, he headed out in his boat, and I wandered back home, trying to figure out how to build a trap for the octopus that was eating our chickens. From Granddaddy's description, it would have to be pretty big. A couple feet long, at least. I grabbed an axe and saw from the woodshed and got to work right after our midday meal. Took me all afternoon to fix up the dad-blame thing, and I stole a couple pieces of fried chicken from the pantry when me wife weren't looking to use as bait. Then I set me up a place in front of the chicken coop, jest like Old Man Hudson, to wait and watch for the chicken thief. My stool was right against the wall so I could lean back if I got tired, and my rifle lay across my knees. Under my stool, I'd placed a dark lantern. It was all lit up inside, but you couldn't see the light unless I opened up one of the sides to let it out.

It was a long wait. I'd jest about fallen asleep on my stool when I heard a stealthy swishing sound coming from the place where I'd set the trap. My eyes were adjusted to the dark by then, and there was a sliver of a moon peering out from behind the clouds. Just enough to see something snaking out from the shadows and pushing its way through the door of the trap to grab the fried chicken, jest like that! The door swung down as soon as the chicken was pulled away from the floor, but it hit the top of a giant tentacle and could go no further. A moment later, the tentacle slid back out the way it came and disappeared into the shadows.

I sat there with my mouth agape. Jehoshaphat, but that tentacle was huge! A foot around, at least! This weren't a little ol' tree octopus. This was one of them giant squid creatures like the ones you read about in them Jules Verne books me wife favors. I sat as still as I could, shaking like a leaf, remembering them pictures of the Nautilus going down under the tentacles of a giant squid. It wrapped right around them sailors . . .

I could feel the liquid eyes of that great big invisible octopus sizing me up. Maybe for his next meal? Then I shook my head. This critter liked chickens. No way was it gonna try to eat a grown man. I raised my gun and pointed it toward the shadow where I'd seen the tentacle disappear. "You stay away from my chickens, hear?" I said, thumbing off the safety. Behind me, I heard a couple of startled clucks inside the coop that broke off immediately. I jammed open the dark lantern I'd kept beside my chair and rushed inside.

At the very back of the henhouse were two empty nests where live chickens had been just a moment before. A single white feather hovering in the air was the only sign of where they had been. It drifted slowly from side to side as it made its way toward the floor.

I blinked as I watched the feather, thinking, *Hoh, boy. This is one very smart, very fast tree octopus.*

All around me, startled hens fluffed their feathers and blinked their beady eyes in the sudden light of my lantern. Outside the coop, something caught the leg of the stool and tipped it over with a bang. There was a final slither and swish, followed by a breathy "heeesh, heeesh, heeesh" that sounded suspiciously like a tree octopus laughing.

Make that a very smart, very fast, very cheeky tree octopus.

Now I was as mad as me wife. How dare that creature steal my chickens and knock over my stool! And the dang thing had laughed at me. That was it! I was going octopus hunting.

The next morning, I went down to the fishing settlement and bought me a huge net. I hung it in the trees by the chicken coop and disguised it with lots of moss I'd harvested from the local trees. Then I built a slightly bigger trap, put some chicken in it, and set it up underneath the big net. If the tree octopus was going to be cheeky, then so was I. Two can play at that game.

I set up my stool in the exact same place after dinner and sat on it with my rifle on my knees and the dark lantern underneath, waiting for the chicken thief to arrive. I waited and waited. And waited some more. It was almost midnight when a large tentacle smashed right into the trap and wrapped itself around the chicken leg I'd left there. Immediately, I opened the dark lantern and twitched the rope holding the net. It came down with a crash, right on top of a huge gray-green mass hunched up at the edge of my yard. It started thrashing about in the light of the lantern, and suddenly the tentacle in the trap retreated and started pulling and yanking at the net. The critter stood up on all eight tentacles—up and up a good seven or eight feet. The rope of the net was draped all around it, but it wouldn't take long for it to struggle free. It turned toward me, and I saw luminous, liquid dark eyes staring at me from inside the net.

"You stop eating my chickens," I shouted, jumping up from my stool and aiming my rifle at the beast. But somehow, I couldn't shoot it. I guess I'm just a softy, like my Granddaddy. It was such a magnificent, improbable critter. Instead, I took a couple of steps forward and gave it a mighty thwack with the butt of my rifle. The tree octopus jumped and scrambled sideways on its eight legs.

"No . . . more . . . chickens . . . " I said again, and gave it another thwack. The creature opened its beak and made a funny sort of hissing sound, almost like the whine of a dog.

"You stick to squirrels," I told it firmly, raising the butt of my rifle again. It squealed and scrabbled backward with all its might, tripped over a large tree root, fell into the ferns at the edge of the forest, and then raced away sideways like a crab, net and all. I waited until the slithering and crashing sounds had stopped. Then I took up my spot on the stool and dozed by the chicken coop until dawn, just in case the tree octopus got any more sneaky ideas.

In the morning, I jogged into the forest and found the rope net about a hundred yards in. Hadn't taken the critter long to divest itself of its trap, once it got away from me and my light. I hurried back to the yard to count chickens, but there were still the same number as there had been the night before. Good.

All was quiet for one week, then for two. No more chickens disappeared from the settlement, so I guessed I'd frightened the tree octopus off for good.

At the end of the third week, I packed a knapsack for myself and headed out into the woods with my fishing pole. I'd thought a lot about the tree octopus in the last few weeks, sort of measuring the distance between the locations it had been

TREE OCTOPUS

raiding and matching it against the layout of the forest. I made my way slowly into a thick grove of moss-laden trees that lay at the midpoint between the homesteads. It was near a fast-running stream, quiet and private and filled with the insects and little creatures that were the natural food of the tree octopus. I sat down at the base of the biggest of the trees—a double Douglas fir—that towered hundreds of feet high. I laid the knapsack full of fried chicken across my knees and leaned back to look up at the twin trees. More than halfway up, there was a large hammock of moss that almost looked like a giant squirrel's nest. It sort of hung along the thickest branch stretching between the trunks of the twin Douglas firs. Just below it, I thought I saw a brown and green mottled figure wrapped around the tree trunk, although it might have been a trick of the shadows cast by the flickering sunlight.

Leaving my knapsack at the base of the tree, I wandered to the stream with my pole to do some fly-fishing. Out of the corner of my eye, I caught a brief glimpse of a dark, liquid eye peering at me through the moss-covered branches. As soon as my back was turned, I heard a slithery sound and a slight whoosh as my knapsack rushed skyward. A moment later, it fell to the ground with a very soft thud. I waited a couple more minutes, making a few more casts with my line, conscious all the while of a pair of eyes watching me from on high. Then I headed back to my knapsack under the tree. It lay upside down on the ground.

"Hey," I said loudly as I bent to pick up my knapsack. A watery black eye appeared through the mossy branches and watched me fishing around inside the now-empty sack. "Who took my fried chicken?" I exclaimed in mock surprise.

Above me, I heard a breathy "heeesh, heeesh, heeesh" that sounded suspiciously like a tree octopus laughing. Then, with a whoosh, the chicken thief scuttled up to the mossy hammock that was its den and disappeared.

16

The Draug

Old Jorgen was thin and wiry and could still do a full day's work on the boats without complaining. So I hired him when young Ole broke his arm a week before we were due to sail. It was April, and we were taking the schooners up to Alaska on behalf of the newly formed Pacific Coast Cod Company. I'd spent most of the winter hiring a good crew for the summer fishing, and the loss of young Ole at the last minute was troublesome. But old Jorgen would fit the bill nicely—or so I thought at the time.

Our schooner had been originally used in the lumbering trade, but we'd modified the *John A* for fishing—removing the donkey engines to allow for more room to hold the cod fish. It also gave us increased bunk space for the fisher crew (the men who took out the fishing dories) and for the dressing crew (the men who processed the cod the fisher crew caught).

It took us thirty days of sailing to reach the cod banks that first year. The cod banks were relatively shallow areas of water where cod schooled. Every morning at four thirty, the fisher crew would row out alone in their dories. They fished all morning and then returned to the schooner for the midday meal. A second round of fishing followed in the afternoon, with the dories returning at around five o'clock.

It was obvious right from the start that old Jorgen knew how to catch cod. Day after day, he'd row up to the schooner for the midday meal with his dory filled to the rim with fish, and it would be full again when he came back in around five. The other fishers regarded him with awe and some jealousy. The jealous ones murmured that old Jorgen had a deal with the Devil that made him such a good fisher, but I quickly squashed their talk. It was bad luck to say such things anywhere—and worse aboard ship where we were always at the mercy of the wind and the waves.

It was old Jorgen himself who told me a little bit about his unusual luck, one stormy evening after a good day of fishing was interrupted by a heavy squall. He knocked on the door to my quarters, and when I answered, he came inside, rolling expertly with the deck as it bowed and bent with each massive wave.

"Evenin' captain," he said to me. "Would you mind a little company?"

I respected old Jorgen and waved him to a seat. Rolling just as expertly across the wave-tossed floor, I got him a drink and then sat down opposite him. We drank and talked casually about the bad weather and the day's fishing. I waited patiently through it all, knowing old Jorgen would eventually get to the reason he'd sought me out on this stormy night.

"Well, captain," Jorgen said after swallowing down the last of his whisky. "I've got a story to tell you. Two stories, in fact. The first one happened many years ago, and the second one happened today."

He paused and held out his glass, which I filled. Then the old man continued.

"I come from the old country, you know. From the north of Norway. We've always been a fishing folk, my people. And sometimes . . . " he gave me a wicked grin, "sometimes the men in our family would go a-Viking. This was back in the old days, mind. Long before my time."

I nodded in understanding. My kin had also gone a-Viking, back in the old days.

"Well captain, my family has always been close to the sea and its creatures. They say my great-grandmother was a *selkie*—a seal-woman who married my great-grandfather after he found her bathing in human shape and stole her seal skin. That's what they say, anyway. All of her children and grandchildren have been expert swimmers practically from birth, so it may be true. My own grandda, he once met a *fossegrimen*—the spirit of the waterfall who lived in the river near our home. The *fossegrimen* liked my grandda and taught him to play the fiddle so sweetly that folks from all the surrounding towns would come to hear him play."

Old Jorgen took a reflective swallow of his whisky, which sloshed in his glass to the rhythm of the swelling sea. Outside the wind roared and the rain beat down on the schooner. It was a terrible night to be out. But inside the cabin, there was a strange stillness as the old man told his tale.

"Every member of our family seems to have some kind of spirit guardian," old Jorgen continued. "When I was twelve, I found a small boy trapped underneath a large rock that had fallen from the side of the cliff. His leg was caught by the heavy stone, and the tide was coming in fast. I found a stick to use as a lever, and managed to move the stone enough for him to crawl out. That's when I realized that it wasn't his leg that was caught—it was his tail. He was a *marmæl*. What the English would call a merman. Well, he looked like a child, but he thanked me with the words and dignity of an adult and said he would send me good luck all my days and warn me of storms that might threaten my ship. And that's exactly what he did. You may have noticed my good luck with cod?"

I nodded and topped off his glass. Oh, yes, I had noticed.

"Well, it's been like that ever since the day I rescued the merman," old Jorgen said. "And that's the end of the first story. And now I'll tell you the second."

His old face grew grim and sad, and I sat back in my chair thoughtfully. I sensed at once that it was this second story that had brought the old man to my door this stormy night.

"You might think my family has been blessed, over the years, knowing all kinds of water spirits to guide and protect them," Jorgen began, after swallowing his whisky. He set the glass carefully in the center of the table where it would (possibly) not slide too far under the roll of the waves. Then he continued.

"But the truth is, my grandmother's people—the seal folk— set a curse against my great-grandfather and against the eldest male from each generation following him. One day the *draug* would come for them, riding in his half-boat, his body dressed in oilskins and his face made of seaweed. And the *draug* would haul each man into his embrace and drag him down and down to the bottom of the sea."

Old Jorgen swallowed nervously and tugged at the ragged ends of his coat sleeves. "My great-grandfather drowned in the sea the day after he saw the *draug* following his ship. He told my great-grandmam he'd seen the creature out of the corner of his eye, following the boat like a vulture waiting for a sick reindeer to die. And before he left in the morning, he gave her the key to the chest where he'd kept her seal-skin locked all the days of their marriage. When news of his drowning came that evening, she unlocked the chest and ran down to the sea, clutching the seal-skin to her chest and weeping all the way.

"My grandma told me that grandda saw the *draug* following his fishing dory in its rotting half-boat, its empty shoulders topped with seaweed that almost—but not quite—made a man's face. The *draug* followed him around for a week, and grandda stopped smiling, stopped eating, and grew thin like a rail. On the seventh day, he fell over the side of his boat on a clear day with no wind and no waves. My da said it looked as if he were pulled over the edge by invisible hands. And he never came to the surface. Drowned by the *draug*. His body didn't wash ashore for nearly a month."

Jorgen rubbed his face with his hands. "Da died at sea too. He was in the Navy and drowned in some kind of an accident. He knew it was coming. The night before he died, he wrote my mam a letter saying he'd seen the *draug* and telling her goodbye."

I stirred in my chair then, wanting to interrupt. Not wanting to hear what he would say next. But he held up a hand and said: "I see you've guessed my news, captain. That old *draug*, he's been following my dory the last two days. You can't see him directly. Only from the corner of your eye. And that's a mercy, really. Dark he is. Sinister. His oilskins roil like the clouds of a thunderstorm, and the empty face . . . the empty face of seaweed draws the eye and makes every hair on my body stand on end. It's wrong—that empty face. All wrong. No eye sockets. No nose. No mouth. And yet I could feel it watching me. Hear it breathing. And almost . . . almost I heard it hissing my name."

Jorgen fumbled in his pocket and pulled out an envelope. "I want you to give my missus this letter, captain. Give it to her with my pay. And tell her I love her more than life itself. Will you do that for me?"

The blue envelope shook in his hands. I tried to say something reassuring, but I couldn't speak for the lump in my throat. I took the envelope and put it into my pocket. Old Jorgen relaxed then and gave me a quivering smile. "Thank ya, captain. Thank ya very much."

He was on his feet then and rolling expertly across the floor to the doorway. A moment later, he disappeared into the storm-tossed night, leaving me to sink thoughtfully against the back of my chair, the envelope rustling faintly in the pocket of my coat.

The storm faded during the night, and the fishers were up at four thirty as usual, heading out to the banks in their dories. I stood on deck and watched them rowing out to their favorite fishing spots. My eye was on old Jorgen. I was afraid his family stories would make him careless, but he seemed all right to me. Then I realized that I was seeing two dories out where old Jorgen had settled down to fish. The second one was strange, crooked somehow. Even from this distance it looked warped and wrong. With trembling fingers, I pulled out my telescope and trained it on the second dory. But it wasn't a dory. It was an old Viking ship with rows of oars on each side. Or rather on one side. It was torn in two along the hull, and the man inside it was wearing oilskins that were so black they sucked at the eyes like a bottomless hole full of nothingness. And where the head should be there was only a gruesome clump of seaweed that seemed to watch you with no eyes, breathe with no nose.

"Jorgen," I gasped. I'd meant to shout his name, but the lump was back in my throat. I swallowed it down and shouted "Jorgen!" as loud as I could. My shout brought the crew running to the rail, but by then it was too late. As I stared mesmerized through the telescope, the oilskin arms reached out of the half-boat and tapped the old fisher on the shoulder. Jorgen turned to face the *draug,* and it pulled him into its foul embrace and hauled him out of the dory and into its boat, which immediately sank beneath the swells and out of sight.

Around me, the sailors gasped. All they'd seen was Jorgen's body pitching over the side of his dory. "Man overboard," the mate shouted, and others took it up immediately. The fishers in the closest dories heard the cry and took it up, and the men hurried to the rescue, searching the fishing banks for hours for the missing Jorgen. I didn't try to stop them. How could I explain that the search was futile? That I'd seen Jorgen pulled into the sea by a *draug?*

It was many hours before the men in the dories and the sailors aboard our schooner gave up the search. Jorgen was gone. Presumed drowned. We held a service for him the next morning. And then the men went out in the dories to fish the banks. There was nothing else we could do.

In September, we sailed back down to the sound to deliver our fish to the processing plant in Poulsbo. The *John A* brought in more than 162,000 cod on that first journey. I lived in Poulsbo, and so did old Jorgen. So after I paid the crew and sent them home, I took Jorgen's pay and his letter home to his old wife. I didn't have to say much. My face said it for me.

THE DRAUG

She was a tough old girl who took the news stoically in front of a stranger. But I saw the tears in her eyes and the way she unconsciously cradled the unopened letter to her chest as she thanked me and sent me on my way. The youngest daughter still lived at home, and I saw her cross over to the sofa and hug her mother as I left through the front door.

I hesitated on the doorstep, wondering whether I should tell Jorgen's wife about the *draug* I'd seen. Then I shook my head and quietly closed the door behind me. Old Jorgen's letter would tell her all she needed to know. Why burden her with anything else? I only wished I could erase the vision from my own mind. But I still saw that seaweed face in my nightmares, and I probably always would.

As I turned my steps toward home, I was suddenly thankful that my family—though they may have gone a-Viking in the long ago—had never messed with *selkie* women. It may have made old Jorgen's family good swimmers, but I thought the price the selkie extracted was too high to pay. Much too high. I shivered at the thought and hurried away, glad to be going home at last.

17

Flying Saucers

MOUNT RAINIER

The pilot cleaned up the last of his equipment, nodded amiably to the man from the Central Air Service with whom he'd been chatting, and headed out to his plane. By trade, he was a fire equipment salesman, and his task in Chehalis that morning of June 24, 1947, had involved installing fire control equipment at the CAS. Now he was headed to Yakima for his next assignment. But he thought he would make a detour over Mount Rainier on his way across the Cascades. According to the CAS man, a C-46 marine transport plane had crashed in that vicinity, and anyone finding the wreckage would earn a $5,000 reward. That money would come in handy, the pilot decided. It was definitely worth a small detour.

The pilot took off from the runway and headed up into the beautiful morning. The day was clear, and he drew in a breath of satisfaction as he gazed upon the lovely view of the Cascade Range. He headed toward Mount Rainier and the possible $5,000 reward, smiling happily to himself and humming a tune in the back of his throat.

The pilot was making a 180-degree turn over the town of Mineral when suddenly he was half-blinded by a huge, brilliant flash that rebounded off the surface of his plane. "What the heck is that?" he shouted aloud in shock. He searched the skies around him for the source of the brilliant flash, but there was nothing to be seen save a single CD-4 flying off to the left and rear. It was too far away to be the source of the light he'd seen.

Suddenly, the brilliant light flashed again. The pilot jerked his head and saw that it came from the region of Mount Baker, nearly one hundred miles north of his current location. Blinking his eyes rapidly to clear them of the floaters caused by the bright flash, the pilot saw that nine strangely shaped aircraft were soaring toward him at an incredible speed, skimming lightly across the tops of the Cascade Mountains. Their flight path would take them right in front of his plane.

Good lord, but they're fast, the pilot thought to himself, drawing a steadying breath. He wondered what kind of planes they were. Jets of some sort. Had to be. Probably military. Though their formation was an unfamiliar one.

The aircraft were closing in on the snow line of Mount Rainier when the pilot realized that they had no tails. None at all. He blinked in surprise and felt the hairs rise on the back of his neck. No tails. So they couldn't be military jets. Then what were they?

The lead craft was at a higher altitude than its followers. It appeared to be crescent-shaped, with a dome midway between its wings. The others were flatter and had a reflective surface. Blue flashes of light sparkled off them from time to time as they erratically tipped their wings from side to side. It was like watching speedboats navigating rough water. The pilot wasn't sure if the blue flashes were caused by the sun or by lights inside the objects. He watched the aircraft with an uneasy fascination

FLYING SAUCERS

that was almost fear. He'd never seen or heard or read about anything like them.

The strange crafts swiftly reached the high plateau between Mount Rainier and Mount Adams. The pilot was keeping one eye on his instrument clock as he watched the flying formation, stunned by its speed. The group of flying objects split into two sections over the plateau. One section continued following the plateau toward Mount Adams, while the second disappeared under the ledge. They reunited on the far side of Mount Adams, rising higher and higher until the pilot lost sight of them in the distance.

Glancing at his instrument clock again, the pilot did a few quick calculations in his head and realized that the strange flying machines had been traveling at approximately 1,350 miles per hour. That was twice the speed of any plane being piloted in 1947—even those flown by the military! The pilot was flabbergasted.

He drew in a deep breath and let it out. His hands were shaking, and he felt goose bumps rising on his arms and legs. There was something very strange about what he'd seen. Something almost . . . otherworldly about the aircraft. He shuddered a bit at the thought, and then laughed at himself.

But somehow, the sight of the strangely shaped aircraft drove all thought of his salvage mission out of his head, and he turned his own plane toward Yakima. After landing at CAS, he sought out a few acquaintances and told them about the flying ships he'd seen, hoping that relating the strange story would help erase that moment of unearthly fright that had filled his mind when he realized how fast the crafts were flying. Unfortunately, not one of them had ever heard of jets such as the ones he'd described. The pilot wasn't sure if that made him feel better or worse about the eerie sight.

The next leg of his journey took him to Pendleton. When he arrived, to his surprise, he was met by an excited crowd who had been informed by the CAS employees about his experience. The pilot was inundated with questions, and he wracked his brain trying to explain the unexplainable to his listeners. "They flew like a saucer would if you skipped it across the water," he said finally, this being the best analogy he could come up with to describe the erratic behavior of the strange aircraft.

He was not surprised that the strange objects were quickly labeled as aircraft from another world. Ever since the Jules Verne novels, folks liked to talk about aliens and creatures visiting Earth from the moon and other planets. But he was surprised at the way journalists seized on the news. "Flying saucers" was the label that the newshounds gave the alien aircraft, and the name stuck.

Having had his ten minutes of fame, the pilot was glad to return to his nice, peaceful home, where the only alien creature within miles around was his neighbor's dog. He'd had enough of flying saucer sightings—at least for a little while!

18

The Miser

TACOMA

In many ways, he was a wise man; the very best of hunters, and a good fisher too. But he loved *hiaqua* more than he loved hunting and fishing. More even then he loved his wife and family. And that was not good. Not good at all.

In the days before the white man came to the Nisqually land with their forts and their guns and their beads, the people traded for goods using beautiful shells from the northland. The name for these shells was *hiaqua*—and the people treasured them and used them in the same way that modern man uses money.

The hunter traded everything he could for *hiaqua*: Every deer and salmon that was not absolutely necessary for survival was traded for the precious shells, and he would not even spare a few of them for his wife to use for jewelry. Instead, he hoarded them and always sought more. He would not attend the feasts held by the tribe each year to celebrate the spawning of the salmon, for he held that such trivial events were wasteful and caused the people to spend the hard-earned *hiaqua* that they should be saving.

The hunter knew all the best places to fish and find game, even in hard times. And so when other families grew hungry, they would come to him and trade *hiaqua* for the meat and fish he stockpiled at home. The hunter was greedy and charged high prices for his food-supplies, even to the poor widows who could ill afford it. He had no time for the poor and needy. He had time only for *hiaqua*.

As the days passed, the hunter grew increasingly obsessed with the beautiful shells. He wanted more and more of them, and his stockpile grew so slowly. So he began to pray to the spirits, begging them to show him how he might obtain more shell money.

At first, the spirits were silent, and the hunter grew angry with them. But he persisted in his entreaties until they grew tired of the endless repetition of his request, and the elk spirit finally told him that a great treasure of *hiaqua* lay on top of Tacobud—the snow-capped mountain that loomed over their land. The elk spirit gave the hunter exact instructions on how to reach the place where the treasure was buried and what to do to obtain it.

The hunter was elated. True, none of his people had ever climbed to the top of the massive mountain, for it was known that the snows above the treeline were the home of the spirits. But the hunter did not care. His lust for the lovely *hiaqua* drove him onward. Packing dried elk meat and camas bulbs, his bow and arrows, two shovels made of elk horn, and his stone smoking pipe, the hunter set off for the mountain after bidding his wife a casual farewell.

He climbed for two days and two nights, up to the snowline of the huge mountain. He dared not make a fire, for he did not want any of his people to see it and follow him. He did not want to share the mighty treasure that awaited him at the top.

Shivering with cold, he waited until the moon rose on the second night to cross into the land where the spirits lived and make his way toward the massive peak above him. He trudged over the snow fields, following the elk spirit's directions and occasionally looking down toward Whulge, the great inland sea along which he had spent so much of his life hunting and fishing.

The peak of the great mountain was just shading pink and golden in the rising sun when the hunter saw the place where the treasure lay buried. It was a huge crater surrounded by white snow. At the center was a deep lake, its waters appearing black against the white snow and purplish rock that surrounded it. On the far side of the silent black waters stood three massive stones—one shaped like a camas bulb, one shaped like a salmon's head, and one shaped like an antlered elk head. It was just as the elk spirit had described.

Joyfully, the hunter skipped and hopped and slid down into the crater and made his way toward the three stones. At last, the treasure would be his! According to his spirit-guide, the treasure lay buried beneath the third stone that bore the appearance of the elk. And it was his for the taking. Ignoring the cold, the hunter slid to a halt beneath the huge stones and pulled out the two shovels he had made from the horn of the elk. He sought then for the best place to start his digging. If he chose the wrong spot, he might miss the treasure entirely.

As he paced around the elk-stone, the hunter gradually became aware of the sinister silence around him. Nothing moved, nothing stirred, not even the wind. The surface of the black lake was completely smooth, like glass. The hunter was not used to such a living silence. In the woods of his homeland, small creatures, buzzing insects, gusting wind, and rustling leaves made a continuous backdrop of noise. But here, there were no sounds at all save the ones he made himself. And there was something strange about the shadows cast by the stones in the light of the rising sun. They flickered and writhed as if the massive spirit-stones were moving, and yet nothing stirred in this mute, silent realm of the spirits.

The hunter paused in his pacing for a moment, his skin prickling. Then he shrugged, took up his shovel, and struck deeply into the snow at the base of the elk-stone. Immediately, he heard a puff-puffing sound coming from the lake behind him. He jumped, chills racing across his skin, and whirled. His hand was already reaching automatically for his bow and arrows. Then he saw, rising up from the black waters, the head of a huge otter-spirit, four times as large as any otter he'd ever seen. The spirit climbed out of the black lake and fixed its dark eyes on the hunter who dared intrude upon its sacred ground. It hit the snow with its huge tail. Immediately, a second otter came forth from the lake, followed at carefully spaced intervals by ten others.

The hunter swallowed hard. The spirits were here, just as the old stories had warned. What would they do to him? Part of him wanted to flee, but his desire for *hiaqua* was so great that it swamped his fear. There was treasure here for the taking, and it would require more than the presence of twelve otter spirits to hinder him. Deliberately, he turned his back on the spirit-creatures, leaning calmly on his shovel as the otters walked toward him single-file and formed a ring around the elk-stone. The lead otter leapt up until it was perched in the antlers of the great spirit-stone, and it slapped the nose of the elk-stone with its tail. When they heard the tap of the tail, the eleven otters surrounding the hunter puffed out once with an eerie "whoosh" sound that made the hunter's stomach roil with fear. But he kept his face set and started digging again in the snow under the sacred spirit-stone, ignoring his strange companions.

Upon every thirteenth stroke the hunter made, the chief otter slapped his tail on the stone, and the ring of eleven otters struck their tails on the snow, causing a hollow ringing noise to echo and reecho over the sinister black waters of the lake. When the otters' tails slapped the ground, a strange electric pulse stabbed through the hunter, making his forehead throb and his vision go blurry for a moment. He paused each time and took a deep breath to clear his sight. Then he kept digging.

He cleared several layers of snow and ice from the base of the stone and then he found himself digging in rocky soil. It was hard work, and his head was throbbing continuously now from the repeated pulses that came with the striking of the otter-spirits' tails. But when he tried to stop for a rest, the otters slapped at him with those same tails, forcing him to continue his heavy work. When his spade broke, it was the lead otter that retrieved the second shovel from his pack and handed it to the hunter.

Bruised, numb with cold and fatigue, and with a strange ringing in his ears, the hunter continued to dig in a strange dream-state in which his hands worked automatically but his mind drifted elsewhere. The ring of otters had drawn so close to him that he could feel their spirit-breath crawling on his skin.

After what seemed an eternity to the sweating, feverish hunter, he uncovered a big, flat, square lid made of stone. With a great effort, he lifted the stone lid up and found that it covered a large hole. Gasping for breath, the hunter stared down into the space below. To his immense delight, he saw great piles of *hiaqua* reaching almost to the top of the hole. In a moment, his fatigue was forgotten. He even forgot his otter-spirit observers as he knelt at the edge of the hole and thrust his arms deep into the tiny, perfect white shells that were strung together on strings made of elk-hide. His hands could not reach the bottom of the hole, so deep was the shell-money buried there.

Cackling with pleasure, the hunter filled his bag with the money, fingering the white shells on their hide-strings with greedy delight. He strung *hiaqua* around his waist, his neck, his arms, his legs. Anywhere he could carry *hiaqua*, he did. And still, the hole seemed filled to the top. Obviously, he would have to come back for more. But he had enough for now.

Carefully, the hunter replaced the cover over the treasure hole under the sacred elk-stone, watched by the dark eyes of the giant otter-spirits. Then he packed snow around it until the place was smooth, and no prying eyes could discern where the treasure hole had been. The hunter wanted no one else taking the *hiaqua* that was rightfully his.

"Mine, mine, mine," he hummed to himself, and he turned toward the edge of the crater and made irritated, shooing motions at the giant otters who still stood in his way.

The otters stood still as statues as the hunter made his way out of their circle and headed along the shore of the black lake toward the crater's edge. They watched until it became evident that the greedy hunter would not turn back, would not remember his duty to the spirits, would not make an offering of *hiaqua* to each of the three spirit-stones that represented the gods who watched over the Nisqually people and who had told the hunter the secret of their treasure.

As the hunter, weighed down by his treasure, stumbled up and up to the edge of the crater, the lead otter leapt off the spirit-stone and headed purposefully toward the lake, followed by his spirit-brethren. With each step, the otter-spirits made an eerie puffing sound that reverberated throughout the crater. And when they reached the lake, they slid into the black waters and began softly beating their tails upon the surface to create a sheer mist that rose and rose, following the greedy, ungrateful hunter as he climbed to the crest of the crater.

When the hunter paused at the top to look back upon the sacred stones beside the dark waters of the lake, he saw a great mist rising toward him. Below it, blacker even than the lake, a menacing cloud roiled and writhed and stretched fingers toward the surface of the water. And in that instant, the hunter knew that the spirits were in that cloud, and that the spirits were angry.

A great terror seized him. He began to run across the ice-fields, hampered by his heavy burden of *hiaqua* but determined to keep it all, no matter what the spirits did to him. The mist rose, blocking out the sunlight until the hunter was running through a devilish, twilight-green dusk. Around him, the mist writhed with half-formed shapes that flickered sickeningly in and out of focus. Behind him, the black cloud grew larger, throwing forth a mighty wind that threatened to throw the hunter off the mountain. Within the voice of the storm cloud, the hunter heard the spirits shouting: "Ha, ha, *hiaqua!* Ha, ha!" A bolt of lightning hit the snow a few yards from the hunter, sending him tumbling to the ground in a sudden slide of snow and rocks.

Realizing that he had to appease the spirits or die, the hunter threw a handful of *hiaqua* shells into the raging storm cloud. Immediately, the wind abated enough for him to stagger to his feet. Behind the raging noise of the storm, the hunter could hear

THE MISER

the puff-puffing sound of the otter-spirits. The hunter broke into a hobbling run, hoping that the spirits were appeased.

But the storm, having gobbled his first puny offering of *hiaqua*, was hungry for more. "Ha, ha, *hiaqua*!" roared the spirit-voices, and a fearful wind pummeled the hunter from behind. He slid face-down across the ice for a hundred feet before he slowed. Above him, he could feel icy spirit hands plucking at the *hiaqua* strings he wore on his neck, waist, and legs. Gasping, feeling blood trickling from his scraped skin, the hunter stripped himself of his *hiaqua* adornments and threw them into the storm cloud that roiled and roared on his heels.

Again, the storm abated for a moment as the spirits evaluated the worth of the offering. Using the lull to his advantage, the hunter sprang to his feet and ran with all his strength down the snow-covered peak, hoping to exit the realm of the spirits before they stripped him of all his treasure. But he was not fast enough. The spirits, still enraged by his greed, threw a great wind after the fleeing hunter, lifting him right off his feet. Gasping, the hunter threw the last of his *hiaqua* adornments into the swirling finger that lifted him up and up into the toothy blackness above. "*Hiaqua*!" the storm spirits roared. "*Hiaqua*!"

With a final, despairing cry, the hunter emptied his bag and watched the swirling winds carry away the beautiful white shells. A moment later, his body was thrown down onto a snowbank, and he lost consciousness.

A long, long time later, the hunter awoke. He sat up and stretched, amazed at the creakiness of his bones. Above him, he could hear a blue jay shrieking. He looked around and realized that he was back in his camp on the border of the snowline. And the meadows about him were filled with camas flowers.

He blinked in surprise. They had not been here when he made camp the night before. The hunter groped for his bag, hungry for the dried salmon he'd packed. But his bag was gone.

Ah, well. There was more where that had come from, down the mountain. He sighed wistfully and stood up, startled by his creaky joints. He scratched lazily at his head and realized his hair was much longer than he remembered, and so matted that his fingers were caught in the strands. That seemed strange. But the hunter did not pursue the thought. He was caught up in the beauty of the morning and the strange peacefulness he felt in his chest. For the first time in his life, he wasn't thinking about *hiaqua*. Indeed, his obsession with the shells seemed as if it had taken place a lifetime ago and was a foolish thing to be laughed at and rejected in the light of this beautiful morning.

Slowly, achingly, the hunter made his way down the mountain, pausing to drink in the beauty around him. As he walked, he was filled with a longing to see his lovely wife and to have a cozy chat with his neighbors.

When at last the hunter reached the place where his lodge stood, he paused in astonishment. A newer, better lodge stood where his old one had been. And the small trees that had grown nearby now loomed tall and strong over the new lodge. In front of the lodge, a very old woman sat stirring a kettle of salmon over the fire. She was obviously well-to-do, covered as she was with strings of *hiaqua* on her wrists, neck, and waist. In her seamed face, the hunter thought he could make out the familiar features of his wife.

As she stirred the pot, the old woman began chanting.

"My old man has gone, gone, gone.
My old man to the mountain has gone, gone, gone . . .
To hunt the elk, he went long ago.
When will he come down, down, down
Down to the salmon pot and me?"

The hunter felt the first stirrings of joy, somewhere under his breastbone. It had taken him a lifetime to appreciate what he had. But perhaps there would be a second lifetime to make up for it?

"Wife, I am here," he called softly.

The old woman looked up at her weary, matted, tired old husband and her seamed face lit up with joy. A while later, after their first excited exclamations were exchanged, the old wife told her husband that he had been away for thirty snowfalls. During that time, she had gathered camas bulbs and special herbs and had earned much *hiaqua* selling them. So now she was rich and had built the new lodge that he saw before him.

The old hunter smiled at his wife, happy for her success. But to him, *hiaqua* did not matter anymore. Not then, not ever.

In the years that followed his return from the mountain, the old hunter became a great medicine man among his people, showing them the best hunting and fishing places and new ways to hunt elk and spear salmon. He was generous with the poor and needy, and his wisdom was much sought after by all who lived in the shadow of Tacobud, the mighty mountain, and also by those who lived along the great inland sea, for he knew how to make peace with the spirits who lived on the mountain.

19

Mountain Devils

Well, we were working our gold mine in a canyon on the east side of Mount St. Helens when it happened. There were five of us miners—me, my pop-in-law, my brother-in-law, and a couple of friends. We'd first staked our claim in that canyon three years afore then, back in 1921. There weren't no roads along that part of the mountain at the time, so we had to leave our car stashed in a safe spot and walk in to our claim. We built a cabin up on a ledge to shelter the five of us at night. It was a one-room affair with a large fireplace and no windows. There was only room for one big bunk, so three of us had to sleep on the floor. It was a rough life, but that's prospecting fer ya.

I was the first of the fellers to notice the strange tracks in the sandy spot down by the crick where we washed our dishes. They were really big tracks; looked at first glance like a huge man's footprints—if'n, of course, the man was fool enough to walk barefoot over this terrain. They were almost nineteen inches long! And they were off a bit—meanin' these prints had only four toes on each foot.

The other fellers thought they were the prints of some oversize Indian and started carrying their rifles on the way to the mine each morning. Personally, I thought the tracks were left by some sort of mountain devil like I'd heard tell of from some of the settlers living in Kelso. The mountain devil was described as a large, hairy critter that walked upright like a man but had the face and arms of an ape. Strange.

It was a bit creepy working on the mountain those first two years. Bizarre shadows could be seen near the entrance to the mine where no shadows should appear. They looked like shadows cast by enormous, hulking figures that stood just out of sight, watching us work. But whenever one of us broke off work to investigate, there was nothing there. We heard an odd thump-thumping noise like the sound of a hollow drum coming from the woods on our claim. Sometimes, I heard a strange whistling sound, and once I thought I saw a black figure out of the corner of my eye, lurking in the trees near the cabin. But when I looked straight at the spot, it was empty. And occasionally, there were footprints near the cabin or close to the mine. But we never got a good look at what made them prints until we reopened the mine after the spring thaw during our third year of operation.

I don't mind telling you, I was spooked right from the get-go that year. Seemed like the hollow thudding sound followed us wherever we went, as if a great beast was thumping its chest. And at night, we'd hear a shrill whistling sound coming from the top of a nearby ridge, and then another would answer it from further away. Creepy. There was something out there, and I didn't like it. We started carrying our rifles with us whenever we left the cabin, and I don't mind tellin' you, I stayed close to the other fellows. This was no time to go trekking around by my lonesome.

One afternoon after quittin' time, my pop-in-law Marion and me were walking down to the creek to get some water when

Marion spotted something—a very big something—crouched behind a tree. I was spooked as soon as I saw it. It was tall and covered with long black hair. Had the face and arms of a gorilla, and its ears were a good four inches long and stood straight up.

I sorta froze in my tracks, and my heart clenched so tight it hurt my chest and made it hard to breathe. I was suddenly aware of how far we were from civilization. There weren't no one around to help us if things got rough. Marion had no qualms at all. He shouldered his rifle before I could get a good grip on mine and let off three consecutive shots. Pieces of bark flew into the air with each shot, but I was pretty sure he got the critter right in the head.

We started running toward the place where the body should be, but there was nothing there. I gaped at the empty spot and then saw the critter running away. I aimed my rifle and let off another three rounds. The huge ape-man kept running.

"Mountain devil," I exclaimed. "The folks in town were right!"

Marion was shaking his head. "I know I hit it in the head. It was a clear shot."

I had no idea how the beast managed to survive with bullets in its head, but it had clearly gotten away.

We were spooked by the incident. Told the other fellers about it as soon as we got to the cabin. I was uncomfortable in my head, thinking that the huge gorilla-creature was roaming around our campsite. It scared me worse'n the thought of a bear or a cougar. It was so dern big, and if it got mad . . . well, the thought made icy chills run up my arms.

Apparently I wasn't the only one bothered by the thought. The other fellows looked a bit green about the gills too. After discussing it at length, we all agreed that it was time to get out until things settled down a bit. We couldn't reach the place we'd parked the car until after dark, so we planned to close up the mine in the morning and hightail it out of there with our equipment. Decision made, we drew straws to see whose turn it was to bunk on the floor, and then we lay down to sleep.

And that's when the attack began. It started with a huge thud against the side of the cabin that knocked a chunk of wood right on top of Marion. He gave a yell and grabbed for his rifle while I pulled the wood off him. A terrible caterwauling rose from outside the cabin. It was a horrible, shrieking noise that ground over the nerves like broken bits of glass and brought the rest of the fellows bolt upright in their beds. I heard something knock over the woodpile beside the cabin. Marion put an eye to a crack in the logs. It was hard to see in the dark night outside, but after a moment he reported that he could see three large, hairy shapes. They looked like the gorilla-creature Marion'd shot earlier in the day. From the terrible noise they were making, I figured there were probably more than three of them out there.

Then the walls shook as a rock suddenly slammed against them. The wailing, shrieking sounds grew louder, and more rocks hit the walls. A couple came right down the chimney and rolled onto the floor. We took some shots through the gaps in the logs, trying to scare the creatures away from the cabin. It seemed to work. They pulled back, and for a while, things were fairly quiet. Then they'd rush us again, pounding the walls with their bodies and throwing rocks until the rifle shots forced them away.

All at once, we heard the pounding of several pairs of large feet on the roof. At the same time, rocks smashed the logs of

MOUNTAIN DEVILS

the cabin from ground level, and the door shivered under the impact of a tremendous body. Marion and I started desperately firing through the roof while the others huddled next to the fireplace, too dazed with fear to be of any use.

The mountain devils on the roof were scraping at it with large hands, and one of them managed to break through a small section. A long arm covered with black hair stretched down through the hole, groping for an axe leaning against a nearby wall. I gave a shout and plunged forward as the axe shot toward the ceiling. I managed to turn the axe head so it wouldn't fit through the opening and got a firmer grip on it as the creature tugged it up and down in frustration. A moment later, the axe and I fell together to the floor, and I tucked it away under the bunk. I lay gasping with relief. If the critters had gotten hold of the axe, they would have broken through the cabin in no time, and we would be torn to pieces.

The attack lasted all night long. I was shaking with terror the entire time. The shrieking alone had shredded my nerves. I winced each time a rock or body smashed the logs of our cabin, expecting that it would break through the thick logs and let the creatures into our flimsy shelter. But somehow the logs held. We'd built the cabin to withstand the tough mountain winters, and it stood on the ledge that night like a tiny fortress in the deep, dark wilderness.

Sometimes the shrieking would die away for awhile, and we'd relax, only to be buffeted by another assault of rocks. Occasionally we'd let off a shot with one of the rifles, but it didn't help much, because we couldn't see to aim.

I thought I'd go mad a couple of times that night when glowing eyes glared down at us through the small hole the creatures had torn in the roof, or a tremendous crash would bend in the logs until it seemed they must break.

As the sky lightened toward dawn, the attacks got less and less frequent, until they stopped altogether with full daylight. We lay huddled on the cabin floor, shattered in spirit. Finally convinced that it was over, we peeked nervously through every crack in the building to check that the creatures were truly gone before we grabbed our things and made a mad dash for the mine to retrieve our costly gear.

As we made our way toward the mine, we saw another of the ape-like creatures standing by the edge of the canyon, looking out over the river. We panicked. I grabbed my rifle and shot at it, forcing my hands to remain steady. I got it three times in the back afore it could turn its head. The critter toppled head over huge heels down into the canyon and splashed into the swift current of the river.

That tore it, of course. If the mountain devils were mad before, they'd be furious now. There was no way we were going to linger at the mine long enough to retrieve our equipment. We rushed away as fast as our legs would carry us—down to the place we'd stashed the car. There was a ranger station five, six miles from our cabin, and we stopped there first to report the incident to the rangers. Then we hightailed it to Kelso with our bizarre story, hoping to have a good long drink to settle our nerves.

The police and reporters formed a posse shortly after hearing our report and went gorilla hunting. They found the cabin even more battered and torn-up than we'd reported, and they saw more of those huge, four-toed footprints around the site. But they never saw the apes that attacked our camp. They'd escaped into the wilderness and were too wily to return while the hunters were nearby.

After the incident at Ape Canyon, as they later dubbed the place, we decided to abandon our claim. It wasn't worth the risk. I'd rather be poor and alive than wealthy and dead. And the other fellers agreed.

20

Bone Cleaner

DOUGLAS COUNTY

The colors of the lake were black and swirling gray, reflecting the roiling mass of storm clouds overhead. The wind whipped down the coulee with awesome force, forming whitecaps on the black waves and ripples all over the surface of the water. Foam lined the edges of the shore. But still, there was no rain. Just the howling wind, the roaring lake, and the boy.

The boy.

He was crouched on a huge basalt boulder at the edge of the lake, shuddering with cold and fear and watching, watching . . .

Around him, all along the shores of the black waters of the lake, lay the too-clean bones of many animals: elk, deer, cougar, bear, lynx. A cracked elk skull lay in a hollow of the rock where the boy crouched, waiting for his stepfather. Waiting.

His stepfather. Where to begin describing the fearful life the child had endured under his cruel reign? He controlled his new wife with an iron fist, subjecting her to a slavery that the others in the tribe abhorred. But none said a word against it, for the warrior was stronger and richer than other men, and he had the power of that wealth and status behind him. When the boy's older brother rebelled against the cruel stepfather, he shortly met with a fatal accident. His horse, a placid old beast nearing the end of its life, suddenly went crazy and kicked the boy to death. A small pinprick of blood on its shoulder—the sort made by a dart—was the only clue ever found as to why the horse went wild. The stepfather, of course, blamed a fly.

The boy shifted his weight slightly, one eye on the wild lake, one on the land. He could see, strewn here and there, the clean, polished bones of a wolf, and the older, grayer bones of a coyote half-buried in the soil. The bones of dead creatures surrounded this lake. They were everywhere. But the skeletons of the dead didn't frighten the boy as much as what had killed them. The most dangerous creature of all . . .

Smash. The boy started wildly and almost fell out of the cleft of the huge rock where he hid as a giant claw smashed out of the wild, black waves and grabbed at the huge stone, trying to reach him. It was Bone Cleaner, trying to catch him.

The boy peeked out of his hiding spot as the claw withdrew into the water. For a moment, he saw a huge, luminous pair of yellow eyes with strangely triangular black pupils poking up through the wild ripples and whitecaps. Then the monster withdrew into the depths of the lake, waiting patiently for him to make a misstep. It would take only one mistake . . .

The boy swallowed hard and turned to look back down the trail. Surely his stepfather would come. He knew the boy was out hunting alone, and he would not want to miss the chance to do away with him, just as he had done with the boy's sister.

His sister. The boy's eyes filled with tears. She had wanted to marry, but not the elderly man of her stepfather's choice. She had defied him, and he had hit her so hard that she fell over and struck her head on a stone. After that, sister acted like a little child—unable to talk, unable to think. She played with a couple of sticks and a cloth that their mother had made into a doll. Hour after hour after hour. Every day. Until the day the stepfather had smothered her in her sleep, saying that she was useless to them—taking up their precious food and clothing and contributing nothing to the family.

So now his mother was down to one child—him. A little boy, only seven years old. And he had watched as she withered away into herself, all hope gone, blindly obeying her cruel husband. She didn't even flinch anymore when he beat her.

The boy's anger had bubbled over. He was small for his age, but he meant to be the greatest warrior in his tribe some day. And he would start by righting this great wrong that threatened his family.

That morning, when his stepfather had hit his mother because she was late with the morning meal, the boy had rushed forward defiantly, threatening the evil man with his spear. His stepfather was a massive man and had turned aside both spear and attack. But not before receiving a disfiguring cut across his cheek. The look in his dark eyes spoke death for the boy, for their neighbors had seen the fight, and whispers were already traveling around the tribe about the boy's defiance. The two things his stepfather valued most of all were his handsome appearance and fierce reputation. To be disfigured by a mere child was something he would never tolerate. The boy knew this. It was all part of the plan.

A flash of lightning crashed down, singeing a nearby tree. In the blaze of light, the boy saw his stepfather descending into the coulee with his spear, stone knife, and bow. He was coming.

The boy waited until the stepfather was near the bottom of the coulee before he slid out of his hiding place onto the bone-strewn shores of the raging lake. He landed beside the antlered skull of an elk and shoved it impatiently aside with his foot. He heard an ominous splash behind him that had nothing to do with the roaring wind, but he resolutely kept his back to the water.

"You will leave my mother alone," he shouted over the wind, glaring at the stony-eyed, grim-faced warrior rapidly approaching him. The red cut on the warrior's cheek looked livid and painful in the greenish light of the storm. "You will never hit her again, or I will kill you."

His stepfather laughed. He actually laughed. "You are an arrogant, small child who will not live to become a man," he said, his feet crunching on bone as he crossed the grisly beach, his stone knife already in his hand. A thunderous lightning strike lit the scene as he lunged toward the child. The boy dodged and fled down the beach right beside the water, aiming for the big basalt rock where he had concealed himself before. The warrior ran after him but slipped on a bone and went down on one knee among the slapping whitecaps at the edge of the lake.

Instantly, a huge claw snapped out of the water and closed over his leg. The warrior gave a shout of pain and then another of terror as a second massive claw closed over his waist, almost cutting him in half. A wave slapped into his mouth, silencing him, as Bone Cleaner swept him under the waters of the lake.

Gasping for breath, the boy ran away up the coulee, out of reach of the terrible claws. He left his stepfather's spear and stone knife among the too-clean bones on the lakeshore and ran home to tell his mother that they were finally free.

BONE CLEANER

In the morning, several warriors hunting along the coulee found the stepfather's stone knife and spear lying beside the too-clean skeleton of a man that had been ripped in half at the waist. They said it was a tragic accident. The man must have slipped into the lake during the storm and been killed by Bone Cleaner, the lake monster.

The boy listened wide-eyed when the tribe's medicine man came to break the news to the new widow. In parting, the medicine man warned the boy not to go near the lake with its terrible monster. The boy gave the man his promise, one hand closing over his mother's. Mother and son did not look at one another, but the mother gave his hand a tight squeeze as the medicine man left their home.

They were free.

21

The Message

I was sitting in the third boring meeting of the day when the text message came through on my phone. "Call me. Right now!" It was from my friend Deanna, the unflappable. If she said to call her right now, that meant I had to call her right now. I slipped out of my seat and through the door into the wide hallway, my body already tensed for bad news.

Finding a semiprivate corner, I pulled Deanna's number up on my speed dial and called her. I didn't recognize the husky voice of the person who picked up. Strange. Deanna normally didn't lend her cell phone to anyone. Then I realized it was Deanna's voice after all. It sounded low and husky with tears. I felt a shiver pass through me. This had to be bad.

"Deanna, what is it?" I demanded. "What's wrong?"

Deanna started sobbing over the line, and I began pacing back and forth in agitation. Finally, she blurted out through her sobs: "It's Danny."

I froze in midstride. Danny was my exboyfriend and still a close buddy. We'd broken up over three years ago, and I'd set him up with my friend Deanna last July. It was a romance right from the start. They'd just celebrated their one-year anniversary, and Danny had called a few days after that to ask me Deanna's ring size. So I knew a proposal was coming soon.

"Danny's dead," Deanna blurted out between sobs. I choked and leaned back against the wall for support.

"Dead," I said blankly. My pulse gave one huge pound that shivered through my whole body. Then I turned to ice. "Wh . . . what happened?"

"He hung himself," Deanna gasped. "His mother found him when she dropped by his house with some letters and bills that came to his old address. Oh, Jenny . . . "

Deanna broke down completely, almost screaming in her agony of grief. Numbly, I told her I'd call her back and hung up the phone. I couldn't take it in. Danny was so alive. Such a happy person. How could he have committed suicide? It was ridiculous.

Except it wasn't. Over the past few months, he'd fallen into a clinical depression and was on medication to treat it. He'd said that Deanna and I were his lifeline, and we both thought he was getting better. Until now.

I snapped the phone shut, trying to think, trying to decide what to do. But all my systems seemed frozen. I took a step away from the supporting wall, and my legs gave way. I fell onto the floor of the hallway and two of my colleagues, coming down a nearby staircase, raced over to me, exclaiming in alarm. Somehow they got me back to my office and explained things to my boss, who sent me home.

The next few days were horrible. I spent as much time as I could with Deanna, but how do you comfort that kind of grief? She blamed herself for Danny's death as much as I did. We should have been watching him more closely. We should have realized his depression hadn't lifted with the medication. We should have . . . we should have . . .

The guilt was awful. And unnecessary. That's what the counselor told all of us, including Danny's parents. Danny's condition was clinical, and he'd hidden his lack of progress from us. How could we save him from himself when we didn't know he was still suffering? Apparently, the depressed often rallied just before falling completely off the cliff. It had happened to others. But this was no comfort. I'd lost my friend. Deanna had lost her true love. Danny's parents had lost their son. Worse, his parents' religion stated that Danny's soul would not be allowed into heaven because he had committed suicide. So there was no comfort for them anywhere.

The funeral parlor was packed during the viewing. Everyone loved Danny. All his old pals were there—big, tough guys trying not to cry. His coworkers were there in a stunned mass, not knowing what to say. What could you say? His family milled around, their faces blank with grief, with no tears left. Deanna could barely stand, and she clung to all of us, her grief palpable.

In a way, it was a relief to get past the funeral; to ride to the cemetery and put Danny's poor, dead body into its final resting place. The human body can only stand so much pain, so much grief, before it rebels. There were still months—years—of pain ahead. But at least this first terrible phase was over.

I went back to work, and that helped some. But now we were all worried about Deanna. The suicide watch we should have set over Danny was now set over his lovely, grief-stricken girlfriend. She could not stop blaming herself for his death, and she grew thinner and paler by the hour. She seemed to be wasting away, and no amount of counseling could pull her out of it. I was desperately afraid she would catch ill. The least little germ would be deadly when she was in this condition.

About three weeks after the funeral, I dragged myself home after a brutally busy day at the office. Thankfully, it was not my day to watch over Deanna. I wasn't sure I could handle it after the political infighting I'd listened to all day long. I kicked off my shoes as soon as I got in the door and absently turned on the speakerphone to listen to my voicemail as I started dinner. The first call was from my mom. The second was from a friend inviting me to a party. Then the third message clicked on.

"Jenny? Jenny? It's me. Danny."

I froze with a salt shaker in my hand and the frying pan spitting oil into the air. The voice sounded breathless and far away. But there was no doubt in the world it was Danny. He had a deep, gravelly sob in his voice that was the result of throat surgery he'd had as a little boy. I'd never heard that sound in any other man's voice.

"Jenny, I need you to give my family a message. Tell them— tell Mom, Dad, and Deanna—that I'm sorry. I didn't mean to hurt them. It wasn't their fault that I died. I was sick and didn't know it. Tell them I'm all right now. I'm all right. And tell Deanna that I love her. I will always love her."

The frying pan hissed and spat oil at me, burning my wrist. Hastily, I moved it off the burner, my hands trembling with the shock of what I was hearing.

"And Jenny—it wasn't your fault either," continued the gravelly voice on the answering machine. My heart stuttered and skipped and then started pounding hard in my chest. "I know you think it is, but it isn't. You are the best friend I ever had. Don't let this ruin your life. I'm counting on you to keep

THE MESSAGE

going, to keep enjoying all the good things in life. Make sure Deanna does too. I love you both."

There was a long pause, and then the gravelly voice whispered: "Goodbye, Jenny. I'll see you later."

The message clicked off.

"New message . . . " the computer-simulated voice began, but I shut it off quickly, tears streaming down my cheeks. Danny. Oh, Danny.

I leaned against the sink until the trembling in my legs stopped. Then I listened to the message again. And again. It was Danny's voice. I knew it was—knew it in my bones. No one else had that gravelly tone. No one had ever been able to imitate it, although they'd tried. Danny had called me from . . . where? I didn't know where. Heaven? Paradise? I was hazy on the religious details surrounding the afterlife. Wherever it was, Danny said he was all right there, and that was good enough for me.

I knew that Deanna was with Danny's parents that evening. I called the house and asked them to bring her over. When they arrived, I played them the message. Deanna almost fainted when she heard Danny's voice, and Danny's mom started to cry. There was no doubt in any of our minds that we were hearing Danny speak to us. We listened to the message over and over, and each time Deanna regained a little more color, and Danny's parents looked a little less gray.

"It's a miracle," Danny's mother said at last, clutching my hand in hers. "God gave us a miracle to help us through. He let Danny talk to us from beyond the grave."

Danny's dad nodded gruffly, too moved to speak. Tears slid down into his curly, red-brown beard, and he rubbed his dark eyes with the back of his hand to wipe them away.

I recorded the message on my digital voice recorder and burned three copies of it—one for Danny's parents, one for Deanna, and one for me. There was no way I wanted to lose Danny's final message.

Deanna hugged me tightly as they left the apartment. "Thank you, Jenny. Thank you," she whispered through her tears. I was puzzled.

"Why thank me?" I asked.

"For being Danny's best friend," she said. "For being someone he could call from beyond the grave."

She dabbed at her eyes with a tissue, gave me a twisted half-smile, and rushed out after Danny's parents.

When they were gone, I played the voicemail again. "Goodbye, Jenny. I'll see you later," Danny's voice rasped out at the end of the message.

"I'll see you later." It was how we always ended our phone calls. But this time, it meant so much more. There was going to be a later for me and my friend Danny. Someday, after all the living I was allowed to do, there would be a later.

I wiped my eyes and said to the air: "Goodbye, Danny. I'll see you later."

Then I clicked off my voicemail and went into the kitchen to make myself a late dinner.

22

Demon Man

YAKIMA

He came out of the woods while the tribe was harvesting huckleberries. Cunning Fox saw him first. The man was very tall and very broad, with muscles that rippled under his skin every time he moved. His skin was dark brown, and he had long, white hair loose to his waist. And his eyes were red. He made for such a strange sight that little Cunning Fox dropped her basket in surprise and ran back through the bushes and trees, shouting in alarm for her mother.

By the time the strange man reached the tribe, everyone had gathered together for safety, the women and children behind the men. Cunning Fox watched him, her eyes wide with curiosity. His garments were so odd—made of a shiny silver material that glittered in the sunlight. Where had he come from? He was like no man she had ever seen before. His hair was white, so he must be old. But his face was unlined, as if he were younger than her father. How strange.

Cunning Fox shivered and crept closer to her mother for protection. The man was a mystery, and Cunning Fox couldn't take her eyes off him. He couldn't possibly belong to their nation—or any of the other nations that made up their world. Yet he greeted the chief and warriors flawlessly in their own tongue, and Cunning Fox knew that they were impressed by this Demon Man with his white hair and red eyes.

The man came back to their village and shared the evening meal with the chief and his wife. Cunning Fox, who lived close to the chief, kept creeping past the fire to look at him, until the Demon Man laughed and called out to her. Shyly, the little girl went to stand before him, hanging her dark head and staring at the ground.

"Would you like to hear a story?" the Demon Man asked gently as the wind stirred his long white hair. Cunning Fox looked up eagerly. She loved stories. She sat down at the Demon Man's feet and listened as he told her about the World Above the Sky, where a little girl just like her lived among the stars and had many adventures.

"Was she the daughter of a god?" asked Cunning Fox when the man finished his amazing story.

The Demon Man laughed a little sadly. "No, my child. Just a daughter," he said.

He sounded sad, so Cunning Fox bravely leaned forward and patted his knee. It felt bony and hard—just like a regular knee. She relaxed a little at this sign that the Demon Man was made of flesh and blood.

"She is a good daughter," she said firmly, and the Demon Man laughed and agreed.

After that, Cunning Fox and the Demon Man were friends. The Demon Man made many friends among the people, and he was eager to help with the work. The men all liked him and treasured the wisdom he shared. The women were impressed by his good manners and kind spirit. And Cunning Fox and the other children adored him for his stories.

"What tribe do you suppose he comes from?" asked the chief's small son. "Do you think he comes from the sea on the other side of the mountains?"

"I think," Cunning Fox said, "that he comes from the stars."

The other children laughed at her. He was a man, just like their fathers. How could a man come from the stars? That was where the gods and spirits lived. Cunning Fox shrugged and said no more about it. But she thought that Good Daughter was the Demon Man's daughter, and that he missed her, which was why talking about her made him both happy and sad. Many of the Demon Man's stories to the children had been about Good Daughter and her adventures. But he told the adults other stories that both amused them and made them think. Cunning Fox, who listened and observed much more than she talked, had seen the adults slowly changing the way they hunted and harvested after they heard the Demon Man's stories. And the hunting and harvesting went better for the changes.

One day, Cunning Fox fell ill and had to lie on her bed and sleep instead of running and playing, or picking huckleberries with her mother. She felt icy cold and hot at the same time. Her body shook with chills, but her fever rose higher and higher, and her mother and the medicine man hovered above her bed with worried faces that swam in her vision.

She began to see other things, too—monsters that tried to grab her, and her dead grandparents. Once she thought she saw Good Daughter wearing a silver suit and playing among the stars.

Then the Demon Man's face, framed by his long white hair, appeared in her dreams. He gave her something nasty to drink and pricked her arm with a device like a hollow stick made of a strange, shiny metal. Shortly after she saw the Demon Man, Cunning Fox felt better and was able to sit up and eat her food. A few days later, her father wrapped her in a blanket and brought her out to the lodge that had been built for the Demon Man. Her father set her down on the Demon Man's lap, and the man told her a story about Good Daughter who—when she was a grown woman—had found a plant that cured a very bad disease that was killing all the people in her tribe among the stars. Cunning Fox liked that story best of all.

"Where does Good Daughter live among the Stars?" she asked. "There are so many!"

The Demon Man pointed up to a constellation above them and showed her a glittering, blue-white star among the swirling pattern. "That one," he said.

The Demon Man lived with the tribe for almost a year, learning their ways, healing the sick, and teaching the nation through his wise and witty tales. But as the year drew to a close, the Demon Man became very sad and very tired. One day, he told the chief that his time with them was coming to an end. He asked that the tribe take him to the top of a certain ridge so that he could be there when he died. The whole tribe was devastated. They had come to love the Demon Man with his long white hair and red eyes, and they did not want to lose him. But who can fight against death? If the Demon Man—with his gift of healing—could not prevent his own death, then no one could. And so, to honor him, the chief agreed to take him to the place where he wished to die.

The day before the Demon Man left the tribe, Cunning Fox found him standing in the huckleberry field at sunset. She slipped her hand into his and said: "You are going back to the stars, aren't you?"

The Demon Man looked surprised for a moment and then smiled down at her. "Yes, I am," he said simply.

"Will you see Good Daughter?" asked Cunning Fox.

The Demon Man smiled. "I will see Good Daughter."

"She is your daughter, isn't she?" asked Cunning Fox.

The Demon Man laughed. "I see I have no secrets from you. Yes, Cunning Fox, she is my daughter."

"When next you see her, please greet her from Cunning Fox," the child said gravely, using the same formal wording her father used to send messages to his sister in a faraway village.

The Demon Man solemnly promised to do as she asked. Then they walked back to the village, hand in hand.

The next day, the warriors led the Demon Man—dressed once more in his shining silver clothing—up to the mountain ridge. When they reached the place where he was to die, the Demon Man thanked them for their hospitality and wished them well in their future endeavors. Then he lay down upon a large, flat rock, drew a strange, silver bracelet out of his pocket, and tapped it a few times with his fingers. It lit up with three small, round lights—one yellow and two green. When the lights disappeared—all except the yellow one—the Demon Man put the bracelet on his wrist, folded his hands across his chest, and closed his eyes. In a few minutes, he grew very still, and then he stopped breathing. The watching warriors sighed and bowed their heads. The medicine man chanted a prayer over the body of their dead friend, and then the tribesmen left the ridge and started the long walk home.

Suddenly, a bright light flashed in the gathering dusk. The warriors turned as one to stare at it. From high in the sky, a large

DEMON MAN

object streaked down toward the ridge and hovered above it. The great wind from the flying object knocked some of the warriors to the ground. Shading their eyes, the warriors watched the oblong, shining object land on the ridge and figures descend to the ground. They wore the same shining clothes as the Demon Man, and they carefully picked up his body and carried it into the ship. All the lights on the ship flashed brightly once more, and then it rose up over the mountains and disappeared into the darkening sky.

Back at the village, Cunning Fox saw the brand-new star shooting up and up over the mountains, and she knew that the Demon Man was going home to see his daughter. She waved a hand and called: "Goodbye, Demon Man."

Then she sat down on a stump just outside her lodge and watched until the sky darkened and a certain glittering, blue white star appeared among the beautiful, swirling constellations in the sky.

23

Soap

LAKE CRESCENT

It was so easy. He was amazed that it was so easy. At first he had been frightened. They'd had words before, but this time . . . well, it ended badly. For her, at least. And suddenly, he had a serious problem. What should he do? He didn't know what to do! Then he thought of the lake. The lake that—according to the local tribes—never gave up its dead. Ever. After that, it was easy.

He had borrowed a rope from a resort owner, telling him that his beer truck was stuck in the mud. Then he wrapped the body in a blanket, weighed down the ropes, and tossed the bundle into the lake. Bye-bye, problem.

The cover story was even easier. Folks in the area knew that he and his wife had marital problems. It was just a case of showing up disheveled at the sister's place in the evening to ask if she'd seen his wife and then going to her workplace in the morning to report that they'd had a fight, and that his wife had stormed out with her luggage. Within days, the story had taken on a life of its own. According to rumor, his wife had run away to Alaska with a Navy lieutenant from Bremerton, leaving him bereft and lonesome. Folks in town even came up to sympathize with him. It was amazing how easy it was. And now he was free to pay court to the pretty girl who'd caught his eye over in Port Angeles. Life was sweet.

After five months, he sought and was granted a divorce from his missing wife. Then he and his new girlfriend moved to California together. Bliss.

Three years passed swiftly by, and he knew he was home free. He'd chosen the wrong lady last time, but things were looking up at last.

He was humming to himself as he washed his hands in the bathroom sink one morning when his girlfriend called out from the kitchen: "Honey, you've got to see this story! They found some woman floating in Lake Crescent, and her entire body was turned to soap!"

He froze, the bar of soap still clutched in one hand. He laid it down carefully, swallowed a few times. "That's interesting," he called back in a voice that was not quite normal. Forcing himself to remain calm, he rinsed his hands and wandered into the kitchen to look at the newspaper. He refrained—with difficulty—from snatching it out of his girlfriend's hands.

The reporters were calling her the Lady of the Lake. Her body, wrapped in a blanket, had floated up from the bottom of the lake after the ropes holding it down had rotted away. During the time she lay trapped 660 feet below the surface, the cool temperatures of the lake had prevented bacteria from eating away at the body, and the chemicals in the lake had leeched into the fat in her body, turning it to soap. The process was called "saponification" and was thought to have been accelerated because the body had landed in an underground stream.

According to the story in the paper, the soap woman had floated to the surface of the lake, and two fishermen had spotted

SOAP

a five-foot-long bundle with an alabaster foot sticking out of one end. The men had reported their finding to the authorities, who fished it out of the lake.

He stood frozen with the newspaper in one shaking hand. It felt as if all the pieces of the world were crashing around him. The thoughtful reporter had described the Lady of the Lake in detail—five foot six inches, red hair, green wool dress, bruises around her throat, and extensive hemorrhaging in her chest. The fingers and toes were missing, and many of the facial features had worn away. Word for word, it was a description of his "missing" wife.

Something in his expression finally penetrated his girlfriend's chatter. "Are you all right?" she asked. He shook himself, forced a smile, and nodded. He was fine. He placed the newspaper very carefully back on the table and went to the refrigerator to get himself a glass of milk. All the while, his mind was racing. What should he do? At last he decided it was best to do nothing. No one had come forward to identify the body. As long as it remained a mystery, he was safe.

His eye fell on the bar of soap by the kitchen sink. The sight of it made him sick.

He did his best to put the story out of his mind in the days that followed, but it didn't work. Every time he washed his hands or saw a bar of soap in the grocery store, it all came back to him. He watched the newspapers, seeking every nugget of news about the case. Would they identify the body? Would they suspect him? His dreams were haunted at night by the waxy white face of his dead wife. The Lady of the Lake.

As time passed, he began to relax again. Perhaps the mystery would remain unsolved. At least he was far away from it all. His dreams became less fragmented, less tense. But the smell of soap still made him sick.

It was more than a year after the discovery that he dreamed of his wife. Not of the white alabaster lady who had haunted his nightmares, but of the sweet, laughing waitress he'd met in a tavern. In his dream, they kissed and cuddled and laughed as they had when they were first courting. But the figure in his arms had suddenly turned to soap, and he woke with a shout that frightened his girlfriend. He lay trembling from head to toe the rest of the night.

He couldn't bear to touch the soap in the bathroom that morning. Something about its smoothness reminded him of the curved cheek of his dead wife. Inside, he felt as icy as the underground stream that had turned her body into soap. Today, they would come for him. He felt it in his gut. It would be today.

He was calm when the police arrested him. And he put on a good show at the trial, protesting that his wife had been alive when he last saw her. But the evidence was stacked against him, and he was not surprised when they found him guilty of second-degree murder. He went through the whole process in a daze, and it was a relief to have the trial over and done with.

He spent the next nine years in prison in Walla Walla, and the only times he felt truly, horribly alive, from the day he went to prison to the day they released him on parole, were the moments when he took up a bar of soap in the bathroom to wash his shaking hands.

24

The Wax Doll

WALLA WALLA

The year I turned fifteen and my brother turned twelve, my father sold the farm in Missouri and announced his intention of moving to the Oregon Territory. We spent nearly a month packing up our wagon, and I cried when we left our house for the last time. But I was swiftly absorbed into the hustle and bustle of the town of Independence, where our wagon train was gathering.

I was almost but not quite old enough to be married, and I was fascinated by all the young men I saw hurrying around their family wagons in the newly formed train. Some of them were good-looking, and young enough to be of interest to me. As I helped my mother load our own family goods, I kept imagining ways to introduce myself. But I was a shy girl, and I couldn't bring myself to follow through on any of my innocent schemes. In fact, I ducked out of sight any time one of the boys drew near our wagon.

Which was how I met Mitchell Stanton. I was hiding from a very handsome boy who was packing the wagon not far from ours when I bumped right into Mitchell, who was passing by carrying a sack full of potatoes. I staggered backward, almost falling, and Mitchell dropped the sack and steadied me until I regained my balance.

"Easy does it," Mitchell said, smiling down into my eyes. I stared up at him, unable to speak for embarrassment. He had a funny shock of dark hair and green-blue eyes in a roundish face. He wasn't as handsome as some of the other boys, but the way he smiled at me made my heart flutter wildly. When I regained my breath, words simply poured out of me. I apologized six ways to Sunday, and he laughed and made jokes about our accident until I chuckled too.

Somehow, after that, Mitchell always seemed to be passing our wagon on one errand or another, and he always tipped his hat to me or stopped to exchange a few words. Mitchell was easy to talk to, and he made me laugh with his jokes. I was relieved to learn that his family was departing in the same wagon train as ours, and my little brother took great delight in teasing me about the matter.

Mitchell must have been thinking along the same lines as me. Somehow he persuaded his brother—with whom he was traveling—to line up their wagon right behind ours. So we would be neighbors when we headed west on the Oregon Trail. Mitchell's brother was a pleasant, short man with a round belly and a happy chuckle. But his wife, Isobel, was different. She was tall and elegant and standoffish. She seemed to look down upon everything she saw, and she said nothing to Mother and I after initial pleasantries were exchanged. Her manners made me feel shy and self-conscious, and her clothes were so beautiful that I felt awkward in her presence, conscious of my homespun appearance. According to Mitchell, she came from an old seafaring family that hailed from Salem, Massachusetts.

Salem. The name of that town sent shivers down my spine. I was good in history, and I had read all about the old witch trials that had taken place in Salem long ago, when the country was first settled. Looking at Isobel, I could easily imagine her casting spells. Oh, not the wild, arm-waving magic reported at the time. No, her magic would be calm and quiet and absolutely deadly. I shivered and scolded myself for my nonsense. It was quite wicked of me to imagine that Mitchell's sister-in-law was a witch.

The first few weeks on the Oregon Trail were not too bad. I found it much easier to walk than ride, since the road was so bumpy. Mitchell and I often walked together, talking, while Isobel rode regally at the front of the wagon beside her roly-poly husband. Mitchell's brother treated his wife as if she were something delicate and beautiful—something to be cherished—and he spared her many of the heavier chores that Mother and I took in stride. Isobel would tend the fire and cook and do the mending. But other than that, she sat around knitting lace or drawing fancy pictures in her sketchbook while Mitchell and his brother hunted, tended livestock, and did the heavy work.

After several weeks on the trail, Isobel unbent enough to speak to Mother and myself in the evenings after all the chores were done for the night. She discussed fashion with Mother, showed me the lace she was knitting, and commented on the local happenings among those in the wagons nearest to us. I privately wondered what she would do if we were attacked by Indians or overrun by a buffalo herd. I couldn't imagine what such an elegant and aloof woman would do in those circumstances. I was soon to find out.

We were only a week out of Fort Laramie when our wagon train was attacked near dawn. I was roused from my sleep by war whoops and terrified shouts. I sat up, heart thudding wildly as I heard the whoosh and thud of arrows hitting the wagon. Father sent Mother and me under the wagon for shelter while he and my brother took up guns to ward off the attacking tribesmen, who were circling the wagon train on their horses. I saw Mitchell and his brother run out to join them, rifles in hand, and my heart leapt into my throat. Please, God, let them be all right.

I turned to look at the Stanton wagon, wondering where Isobel was and whether I should run out and get her. And then I saw her, standing calmly in the rear of the wagon, one of the black-thread lace doilies she had knitted stretched between her two hands. She was chanting softly, and all the arrows and bullets flying through the air bounced against an invisible wall that surrounded the wagon and fell harmlessly to the ground. I gaped at the sight, goose bumps rising on my arms. So that was why the Stanton wagon had suffered no injuries, needed no repairs after months of hard travel on the Oregon Trail. Isobel really was a witch! I clutched at my Mother's arm, wanting her to see Isobel's magic at work, but Mother's attention was on our attackers, and she didn't even turn her head to look at me. So I was the only one who saw Isobel's spell-casting.

The attack was over almost as soon as it had begun. Some of the men and boys were killed, and we lost more than twenty horses and twice as many cattle. But the Stanton men and my father and brother were spared. The wagon train limped the rest of the way into Fort Laramie and relative safety, and we spent a week there stocking up on supplies and repairing the damage done by the Indian attack. Then we were back on the road.

The Oregon Trail grew harder as we passed over the Continental Divide. Water—and grass for livestock—became scarce. The drier air caused wooden wheels to shrink, and the iron tires that held the wheels together loosened or rolled off. The buffalo herds on which we had depended for fresh meat became increasingly hard to find the farther west we rode. Cooking fuel, whether wood or buffalo chips, also became harder to find.

It nearly broke Mother's heart when we realized we had to lighten the wagon in order to survive the harshness of the trail. We unpacked her precious hand organ, and father left behind the fancy desk his grandfather had carved with his own two hands. But we had to do it to survive. Food and tools were vital; heirlooms were not.

When I wasn't walking with Mitchell or doing chores, I was observing Isobel. She seemed to be surviving the heat and hardship very well. Indeed, I never saw her break a sweat, and I sourly wondered what spell she used to keep herself cool and fresh. She must also be using a spell to keep her family well fed, I figured, for the Stanton stewpot was never without meat, and their supply of food never seemed to diminish.

One night when sleep wouldn't come, I crept over to the Stanton wagon and watched Isobel stirring up a potion. She chanted softly as she worked in a language I didn't recognize. When she finished the potion, she poured some of it into the medicinal flask her husband always carried with him. Then I watched her melt wax and form it carefully into small figures, four men and three women. She spoke certain words over the figures and placed three of them carefully in a small pouch she wore under her apron. Then, without looking around, she said: "Come here, Margaret."

My mouth dropped open in surprise. I was lying on the ground on the far side of the wagon, peering at her through the wheels. How had she known I was there? But of course, the answer was simple. Isobel was a witch. That's how she knew.

Reluctantly, I got up and walked over to the fire. Calmly, Isobel placed the four remaining wax dolls into my hand. "Keep them somewhere safe and your family will be safe," she said.

Then Isobel dipped a ladle into the stewpot and lifted the dark liquid out. "Would you like a love potion for Mitchell?" she asked. I took a step backward, shocked. "N . . . no. Thank you, Isobel, but no," I managed. "I'd rather he loved me because he wanted to."

Isobel chuckled a little. "Romantic, aren't you? Well, it's up to you."

She dropped the ladle back into the stewpot and then turned back to me, a little frown marring her perfect forehead. She said: "I am sorry about your mother's organ and your father's desk. If I weren't such a selfish woman, I'd have made you one of these before." She reached into her pocket and drew out a strip of white lace. "Tuck this into the cover of your wagon where it won't be seen, and you won't have any more trouble."

Then she shooed me back toward my wagon and told me to stop spying on her or she'd turn me into a toad. I shivered and obeyed her. I wasn't sure if she could turn a person into a toad, but I wasn't going to take any chances, just in case.

I put the lace into a secret place in the wagon cover and tucked the wax figures into my sewing kit before I slept that night. It was probably wicked of me to accept gifts from a witch, but I didn't care, as long as they kept my family safe. Besides, she was a white witch. Wasn't she?

Two days later, our wagon train pulled up outside the Whitman Mission. It was wonderful to have a place to rest and get some food, and my parents were glad to talk religion with the missionaries. But Isobel hated it. She went all white and distant, and she treated Narcissa Whitman as if she had a contagious disease each time they met. I had never seen two women take such a profound dislike to each other.

The night before we left, I saw Isobel entering the Whitman's house holding a small wax doll shaped like a woman. Unlike the ones she had given me, it had been dyed black and was run through with two pins—one in the chest and one in the head. Intent on her task, she didn't see me in the kitchen, where I was taking leave of some of the women who lived at the mission. She disappeared into the front room for a moment and then departed again out the front door, so silently that no one else noticed her.

I excused myself and slipped into the front room, hands shaking with fear, convinced that the doll made of black wax was supposed to be Narcissa. I found it cleverly tucked away in a crack and removed it from the house. But I didn't know what to do with it after that. Was it enough simply to remove the doll from the house? Would that break the spell? I was afraid to remove the pins. Without knowing how to break the spell, I might hurt or kill Narcissa instead of saving her. But somehow, I felt like I should do more. Such an evil thing should not be left lying around.

I remembered hearing that evil spirits couldn't cross running water. If that were true, than maybe running water would also neutralize evil spells. It was worth a try. I took the doll to a nearby stream and threw it into the deepest part, praying that the running water would break the evil charm. Then I hurried back to our wagon, hoping that Isobel would never find out what I had done.

THE WAX DOLL

It took all my self-discipline to act normal around Isobel the next morning. I kept remembering the black wax doll and the red pins. Obviously, Isobel practiced the black arts as well as the white. Remembering her husband's flask full of love potion, I wondered how much of her magic was truly good. How could you really know? At least she seemed to like our family, which relieved my mind a little.

The rest of our journey passed without major incident or accident, to the astonishment of everyone save myself and Isobel. Our two wagons passed all obstacles unscathed as we traversed the Blue Mountains and crossed down to the Dalles. The next stage of our journey took place on the Columbia River, and our family shared a boat with the Stanton family. We easily passed over the terrible rapids that had killed so many before us, while the boats to the fore and aft lost both goods and passengers. And then we reached the promised land. After scouting about the Willamette valley, Father decided to settle on the north side of the Columbia River. The Stantons built their home within a mile of us.

It wasn't long after we finished building our new home that we heard the news about Narcissa and Marcus Whitman. Shortly after we left the mission, a measles epidemic broke out. Many of the Indians were killed, while the white newcomers— who already had some immunity to the disease—survived. The Cayuse suspected that the Whitmans and their foreign religion were the cause of the fatal disease, and they killed the Whitmans and eleven other whites and burned the mission down.

I was sickened by the news. Had the disease and the massacre been caused by the little wax doll that Isobel put in the house? Perhaps the charm hadn't been broken by running water? I would never know.

I insisted—when Mitchell proposed and I accepted—that the two of us settle as far away from his family as we could without giving his sister-in-law offense. By the time we married, Isobel had a baby to tend to and another on the way, so she barely noticed our going. Still, I kept my wax doll in my sewing case, and made sure Isobel gave me Mitchell's to keep as well. No sense in taking chances. And after we departed, I made sure to send my sister-in-law at least one friendly letter every few months—just in case.

I never told my husband that his sister-in-law was a witch. And I never told anyone about the black wax doll I'd thrown into the stream, though it gave me nightmares for years. I knew it wasn't my fault that the Whitmans had died. I'd done my best to destroy the evil charm. But somehow, I still felt guilty, and I knew I always would. Which was too bad, because Isobel never did.

25

Beloved Woman

MOUNT ST. HELENS

The mountain came first, rising up in rage and splendor between her two suitors. And then we came, the Seatco monsters and myself—their servant, the Ghost Elk—to live upon her slopes and prey upon the innocent. But perhaps I should start my tale at the beginning . . .

—

In the time of giants, when the world was mired in lava and smoke and fire, there lived a beautiful woman who was loved by two brothers—sons of the Great Spirit. Wy'east, the elder brother, was proud and wished to own the woman, as he would a prized possession. But Pahto, the younger brother, loved her smile, her laughter, and the sparkle in her eyes, and his heart yearned to spend a lifetime beside her. The woman looked to first one brother and then the other, unable to choose between them.

Enraged by jealousy, the brothers fought for the hand of the beloved woman, using earthquakes and lightning and lava the way a normal man might fight with spear, knife, and arrow. So great was their rage that those who inhabited the world at this time feared for their lives, and the mighty bridge that spanned the Columbia River fell with a terrible roar, creating the Cascades.

Furious at the behavior of his sons, the Great Spirit decided to intervene. As he came down from the world above to discipline the brothers, a chance-flung boulder struck down the Beloved Woman over whom they fought. With a cry of terrible pain, she fell to the ground, and Pahto, the younger brother, was stricken to the heart by her injury. He knelt beside her in an agony of grief and fear. In that moment, the dying woman looked into his face and at last knew her own heart. Above them, Wy'east, the elder brother, shrugged and leaned on his spear. The woman was good only as a possession, and he didn't care to possess damaged goods, even if she survived the accident.

The Great Spirit stopped beside the dying woman and cried to the brothers: "Look what you have done." He gestured to the darkening sky, to the ash-filled river, to the desolation around them. "You have destroyed the goodness of this land, and for that you must pay."

With a wave of his hand, the Great Spirit turned Wy'east, standing tall and proud with his spear, into Mount Hood, and placed him on the south side of the great river. Then he turned to Pahto, the younger brother, who clasped his dying beloved to his heart. "Because you loved so well and so faithfully, I will keep you always beside the woman who holds your heart," he said gently. With those words, he transformed the younger brother into Mount Adams, with his head ever bent toward his beloved, and beside him he placed the Beloved Woman, transforming her into Mount St. Helens . . .

—

This is the tale of the beginning that we—who came later—were told by the spirits of the air and sky when first we rose up in this land. And who are we to doubt the ones who move between our world and the world above?

The story of the beginning made many things clear to those of us who came after. The two great lovers have lived together through the centuries, while the ash-filled skies cleared and the animals and trees returned to the land. The younger brother was content to stand beside his beloved and rarely felt the need to play out his passions on the landscape. But the Beloved Woman was entirely different. She was female to the core and as changeable as any of her sex; serene and calm one minute, and spouting fire and rage the next. Yet it was to the Beloved Woman that my masters—the Seatco—came at last to settle in the lovely lake that stood in the shadow of her icy peak. For this mountain was a good place, with plenty of fish and game. And it held sport for my masters, for the native tribesman came there often to hunt and fish. And my masters were fond of human flesh . . .

And that was how I was born. The first thing I saw in this world was the face of the masters, twisted and grotesque; lumpy noses and sharp teeth and too many arms and legs. I looked for beauty in their faces and saw none. But I was beautiful—a pure white elk made from spirit and air. And around me, the sparkling water and heavy forests were also beautiful. It was a good place to be born. I loved it immediately.

Deep under my hooves, deep inside the earth, I sensed the heartbeat of the mountain, the raging fires—banked for the moment—that lived within her. And like Pahto, I too fell in love with the Beloved Woman. With the mountain of fire.

My duties were simple. When tribesmen came into the vicinity, I was to lure them toward the lake, running just fast enough to keep away from their spears. When they forced me into the water, the masters would rise up and snatch them under the waves, making a meal of them.

It was a good plan, and it worked extremely well in the beginning. Some men were foolish, and some were greedy, and all desired my pure-white coat, which would make a fine trophy. But as one generation succeeded another, they grew wary, passing down the tale of my treachery, and over time the Seatco found it more and more difficult to find a human snack.

About this time, the Beloved Woman grew angry and threw plumes of smoke and ash into the air. The skies darkened, and the tribes fled from her slopes in fear. Forests burned, and the glaciers melted away. When she grew calm once more, the land was devastated and took a long while to heal. It wasn't until another generation had passed that the tribes returned to our lakeshore, and by then they had forgotten the Ghost Elk. And so, for another generation or two, I plied my tricks, and the Seatco snatched the unwary from the shores of the lake.

Over the centuries, the pattern recurred. The mountain would erupt and the tribes would flee. When the forest emerged again, new generations of tribesmen hunted the Ghost Elk to the shores of the lake and were eaten by the monsters within.

But then the white man came, and the world started to change. The tribes were driven away from the mountain of fire, and the white man built houses and roads and summer retreats upon the Beloved Woman. The Seatco grumbled among themselves as more and more people came. They didn't like the white man, who honored different gods and disregarded the old ways. It was not long before the Seatco left the shores of their lake, going instead to live in the Salish Sea, near the tribes whose belief had breathed life into them eons before.

They left me behind. I wasn't needed in the new land. Had they asked me to join them, I would not have gone anyway. I could not bear to leave the Beloved Woman behind. With every step, I felt her heartbeat beneath my hooves. I knew her moods— her laughter, her tears, her anger. She was as beloved to me as she was to the younger brother who still stood beside her.

So I wandered the mountain and watched as towns grew upon her slopes. As schoolchildren and gold miners, hunters and hikers roamed her woods. Some even settled upon the shores of the lake where I was born, under the crest of the fire mountain.

I spent most of my time near the lake, showing myself occasionally to the visitors who flocked there, usually in the early morning when the mists were rising from the water. At night, I would creep close to their campfires to listen to the tales woven by those who came to stay on the Beloved Woman. Their stories were strange—different from those I had heard for so many eons around the campfires of the tribesmen, and from those told to me by the spirits of the air. But they were interesting. I learned the name of the machines that flew through the skies overhead and those of the large beasts that spat and growled over the roads. Airplanes. Cars. How strange.

One night, as I listened to the visitors' stories, I felt the heartbeat of the mountain change underneath my hooves. I was puzzled. I was used to all the moods of the mountain, but I'd never felt this one before. Was it anger? Jealousy? I prodded gently at the puzzle, to no avail. It wasn't until I'd trotted almost to the edge of the glacier at her peak that I knew. It was fury. Outright fury. The fire inside the Beloved Woman was raging hotter than I'd ever felt it before, and she was getting ready to burst. Not the mild eruptions of the past few eons. This one would be big.

I was alarmed at the thought. I'd come to enjoy the bustle around my lake, and I particularly liked the children who came there with their scouting camps. Somehow, I had to let them know that the Beloved Woman was angry. Somehow, I had to make them leave.

And so, I began appearing to the children—first at dawn, then at dusk. They exclaimed in fear and delight when they saw me hovering over the water. But they did not leave. I realized that my tactics were wrong. It was the adults minding the children that I should warn. I enlisted the aid of the air spirits, for I found that modern adults did not see me as readily as did their young counterparts. The air spirits whirled around the camps, shouting messages of warning into the ears of every adult they encountered. And I showed myself to all of the adults who had the capacity to see into the spirit realm.

To my relief, the message got through. The children left the lake and did not return. The visitors to the campground left as well. I tried to make the caretaker leave, but he was cantankerous and loved the Beloved Woman as much as I. So he stayed behind.

Then men with strange devices came and settled upon the ridge near the peak. I trotted up there several times, hoping to warn them of the fury of the fire mountain. But they already knew. Their devices were measuring her rage every day, and they sounded excited. It was a puzzle. The air spirits and I discussed it at length, but we could not come up with an answer. Perhaps they wanted to die? Perhaps it gave them some sort of special status in the next world?

Early—very early—one morning, I awoke from my drifting half-sleep, feeling the tension in the Beloved Woman. Today was the day. I knew it. And so did the wild creatures around me, who were already fleeing for their lives. Calling to the spirits of the air, I ran to the caretaker's home and shouted a final warning at him. He did not even stir in his sleep. Then I raced to the ridge to shout in the ears of first one and then another of the men watching the Beloved Woman with their devices. They ignored me. I sighed at the futility of it all and climbed into the sky, rising with the air spirits to a place where I could watch the Beloved Woman explode with rage, as I had done so many times before.

Below me, the earth began to tremble around the magma bulge I had noted on the face of the Beloved Woman. The entire northern slope above the bulge collapsed with a roar louder than thunder. The whole mountain shook as rocks the size of human houses slid down toward the river valley below. Dramatic as this was, the Beloved Woman had only just begun to express the fury within her.

The massive landslide released a hydrothermal blast that punched laterally through the landslide scarp at twice the speed of the sliding hillside. It overtook the avalanche and devastated a fan-shaped area on the northern face of the Beloved Woman. The trees on the first ridge were shattered to stumps, and shards of wood were caught up in the massive steam-blast. On the second ridge, the trees were blown down like matchsticks, and several miles after that, the remaining trees burnt to a crisp where they stood.

BELOVED WOMAN

Meanwhile, the landslide continued down into the valley, partially filling my lake and raising the lake bed more. In an instant, it doubled the size of the shoreline. Part of the landslide sheared off the top of the ridge directly facing the dome, but the rest was deflected by the taller sections and entered the north fork of the river, filling the valley with a craggy and hummocky deposit. The face of my Beloved Woman now had a mile-wide horseshoe crater in it.

A few minutes later, an eruption column arose from the blasted-out summit of the Beloved Woman. It spread into a umbrella region and deposited ash as far as the eye could see. For the next nine hours, the fire mountain spewed ash upward and pyroclastic flows and lahars downward into her valleys. Some of these flows extended into Spirit Lake and down the north fork of the Toutle River. The heat provided by the flows resulted in secondary steam explosions that formed large craters.

The Beloved Woman was giving quite a show, and the air spirits whirled around me, shouting with fear and excitement. But at last, she tired of the display, and the eruption ceased— at least for the moment. My lake was filled with the bodies of dead trees, washed down from the ridges when the avalanche pushed the water up and over them. And the Toutle River was gone. Buried forever beneath the ash and mud and pyroclastic flow. I trotted over the new landscape, unharmed by the heat and debris—for was I not made of spirit myself? My mountain looked completely different, but still she was beautiful, even in the aftermath of her rage.

More than fifty people died on the day the Beloved Woman exploded, including the caretaker and one of the men with devices. They hadn't heeded my warnings. Nearly 230 square miles of forest were blown down or buried beneath volcanic deposits. I listened to the experts who came afterward to study the rage of the Beloved Woman. They said that 250 homes, 47 bridges, 15 miles of railways, and 185 miles of highway were destroyed by her rage that day. And the summit of the mountain was reduced in elevation from 9,677 feet to 8,365 feet. The Beloved Woman was in quite a temper that day!

And for many days to follow. The Beloved Woman continued to grumble and mutter and erupt for many years afterward, while the animals and trees slowly returned to the farther slopes, and people crept in after them. I was glad to see the people come back, but saddened by the change in the lake where I was born. It would regain its beauty in time, I knew, as the fire mountain calmed down. The people would settle by her waters and build cabins. Someday I would listen again to campfire stories and appear before wide-eyed children in the mists of dawn.

I wait for that day with anticipation. And I am not lonely. The ghosts of the people who perished in this last great eruption hover above the lake waters at night, keeping me company in their quiet way. Sometimes, I hear them murmuring to themselves. And sometimes they weep. How long they will stay here, I cannot tell. Many ghosts have come and gone over the centuries that the Beloved Woman has stood in this place. But only one remains here forever. It is me. The Ghost Elk. And I will never leave.

26

Totem

There are two adages my mother completely forgot to tell me growing up. First: Don't mess with other people's gods. Second: Be careful what you buy at garage sales. Either one might have saved me from a truly ghastly experience. But she completely neglected to mention either to me. Maybe she didn't know.

It seemed like your ordinary, everyday garage sale. The house was a split-level sitting in the suburbs of Seattle, and the family members manning the tables were friendly of face and manner. I looked at the racks of used clothes, the battered old furniture, the array of electronic equipment. Then I saw a little black shape half-buried in a box of toys. On impulse, I bent down and picked it up. It was a carving of a totem pole.

I was keenly interested in totem poles and their meaning. This specimen was pure black—the color of power. And it felt old. It was worn in places, as if a number of hands had held it over the years. It was nine inches tall and bore the sharp-beaked face of Raven at the top. At the bottom, I recognized the face of Coyote. Odd to see Coyote and Raven on one totem. They were both tricksters and represented both the good and evil in humans. They also—in various traditions—were said to have

175

created the world. In between the two creatures were grotesque faces and intricate symbols that I had never seen before on any totem pole. The whole carving looked twisted and strange. All in all, it was as bizarre an object as ever I'd seen. I couldn't look away from it.

"How much?" I asked the teenage girl sitting behind an adjacent table.

She glanced at the carving. "That old thing? A quarter."

I dug in my pocket, gripping the carving so hard that the Raven's beak bit into my palm.

"Do you know the history of the carving?" I asked, forcing my voice to remain casual. My heart was beating rapidly in my chest, and for some reason, I tensed, as if the answer would be important. I had no idea why I felt this to be a momentous moment. But I did. The air seemed to crackle around me, and I leaned forward a little to hear every syllable of the girl's reply.

"It belonged to my grandfather," she said in a bored manner. "He collected all kinds of junk from all over Washington. He was fascinated by anything that had to do with magic. That carving is supposed to summon a bird or a coyote—something like that. He told me about it once, but I forget."

Summon a bird or a coyote? What did that mean? I shrugged, thanked the girl, and walked toward my car. Far up in the oak tree overhead, I heard a raucous caw. I looked up into the wise old eyes of a huge raven. "Did I just call you?" I asked it facetiously, feeling the sharply carved beak digging into my palm.

"Caw!" said the raven. It spread huge black wings and flapped away as I got into my little car and edged out of the driveway.

I was about halfway through my week-long summer vacation, and I was spending my last night in Seattle with my cousin Richard—a confirmed bachelor and a sports nut. I parked in his driveway, and we got into his SUV to hit the local sports bar with a couple of his buddies. I was reluctant to leave the totem in my car, so I put it into my pocket and brought it along. I mentioned my new find to Rich as we drove downtown, but he wasn't into totems and changed the subject as soon as politeness allowed.

We spent a terrific evening with the guys, watching baseball and drinking beer. It wasn't until I reached into my pocket for some spare change at the end of the night that I noticed something strange. My fingers brushed the totem in my pocket, and it was ice cold—so much so that it burned the side of my finger. I yelped and pulled my hand out quickly. My finger had a long, white burn mark along the outside edge. It throbbed once and then subsided.

I frowned at my ice-burnt finger and then gingerly reached back into my pocket to touch the totem with the tip of one finger. It was warm. The tiny hairs on my upper arms pricked, and I gave a superstitious shudder. Why had the totem been so cold just a moment before? It was angry cold, whispered a little voice from my subconscious that I'd learned not to ignore. I frowned at the phrase, wondering why I'd thought it. Angry? How could a carving be angry?

We parted with our pals on the sidewalk and headed to the open lot where we'd parked the SUV. As we neared, Richard let out a curse of rage and ran forward. The SUV was parked right under a streetlight, and in its brightness we could both clearly see marks scraped right down the center of its roof and along both sides—as if hoodlums had attacked it with knives or car keys. Or as if giant raven talons had hit it repeatedly, whispered the irritating voice from my subconscious. I told it to shut up and joined my cousin, who'd run to the guard booth and was berating the man within for negligence.

I checked my own little car when we got back to Richard's house, but it was still intact. So much for angry ravens, I jeered at myself, feeling all the muscles in my back relaxing. It was out of character for me to be so superstitious.

Just before bed, I carefully removed the old black totem from my pocket and put it on the bedside table. "Haven't heard from you yet, Coyote," I murmured sleepily, stroking its nose at the bottom of the little totem pole. It was warm to the touch. I turned over and went to sleep.

—

"Look at that! Will you look at that!" I was awakened by an angry shout from outside. I jumped out of bed and threw open the window. All up and down the street, garbage cans had been tipped over, and refuse littered the lawns and sidewalks. Angry neighbors were milling about, shouting at one another about loose dogs—though there were none to be seen. Richard's lawn was just as bad as the rest, and I spent most of the morning helping him clean up before departing on the next leg of my trip, which would take me to a riverside cabin in the Cascades.

I was feeling distinctly uneasy as I slung my suitcases into the car and bade my cousin farewell. Odd that such a . . . doggy . . . display of temper had followed my remark to the coyote face on the totem pole. On impulse, I pulled off the highway and headed toward a used bookstore I liked to frequent when I was in Seattle. It had a fine section on totem poles, Native

American lore, and the occult. I spent an hour browsing and came out with some books on all three topics. It suddenly seemed rather urgent for me to find out what the symbols on my new carving meant.

Tucking the books into the backseat, I drove back onto the highway and headed up into the Cascades. In his will, my grandfather had left a hunting cabin to be shared by the families of his four children. I had arranged to use it for this weekend. A little solitude after the demands of my job. A little living off the land. It sounded like paradise.

I stopped at the grocery store in the last town before my backwoods turnoff and stocked up for the weekend. I picked up some oil (to fry the fish), potatoes, odds and ends, bait, and a new lure for my fishing pole—one that came highly recommended by the chap at the register.

When I stepped back outside, grocery bags clutched to my chest, I saw a huge raven perched on the roof of my car. It gave me a long, measured stare and then fanned out its huge wings. For a moment, I thought it was going to attack me. Instead, it flew away. The marks its talons left on the roof of my car were the same as those that had ruined the paint job on my cousin's SUV. I gulped and got into the car. What was going on?

I reached the cabin at dusk and hurried inside with my grocery bags and luggage. It was too late to go fishing now, so I made a light dinner, built a small fire in the woodstove, and settled down on the couch to read my new books. I set the small totem pole on the table beside me under a lamp, where I could compare the symbols on its black surface to the ones in the books. Then I opened the book on totem poles and started to read. The book was fascinating. I spent several hours paging through it as I drank a couple of beers. Unfortunately, none of the archaic symbols it portrayed appeared on my little totem. I laid it aside and took up the book on Native American lore.

It was almost midnight when a demonic howling began. First on one side of the cabin and then on the other, a mournful cry rose to startling heights, came back down, and began again. Coyotes. A whole pack of them, by the sound of it. So startled was I that I dropped the book I was reading on the floor. My arm brushed the end table, and the black totem pole fell into my lap. It was ice cold, and my thighs went instantly numb. I brushed it hastily off my lap onto the floor, which went frosty beneath it. The howls were coming from all sides now, as if the coyotes were circling the cabin. Hastily, I grabbed for the hunting rifle we kept over the front door. I loaded it with hands that trembled slightly. Then, cracking open a window, I shoved the muzzle through and peered out into the darkness.

A bloated, orange-colored moon was rising over the mountain peaks, casting an eerie light that made the shadows appear gray and purple and dark blue. Spectral clouds glowed in its light and flitted softly across it, changing the light from moment to moment. I saw a huge gray blur race behind my parked car, and I jumped when something howled right under the window. I shot into the darkness in panic—once, twice. But instead of scaring the creatures away, my shots seemed to enrage them. The howling intensified and drew closer to the cabin.

I leapt back from the window, slamming it shut. Then I put the rifle down with shaking hands and dropped to my knees beside the freezing-cold totem lying on the floor. I grabbed it and shouted: "Go away." Instantly, there was silence. I dropped the freezing totem, my hands stinging with pain. Already,

I could feel it growing warmer as the danger passed. "Dear Lord," I whispered. What had I gotten myself into? I staggered to my feet and limped into the bedroom, exhausted.

Things looked much brighter in the morning. I laughed at my midnight fears. It was a simple coyote pack, howling at the moon. Why had I been so freaked out? It was part of nature— one of the reasons I'd chosen to come to this remote cabin instead of spending another three days in the city. I whistled cheerfully to myself as I packed a lunch and set out for my favorite fishing hole on the local river. I would make a day of it and then fry up the fish I caught with some potatoes and have it for dinner. I planned to leave the little totem pole in the cabin, but at the last minute I tucked it into my pocket. I knew it was absurd, but I couldn't quite forget the way the howling had stopped when I'd grabbed the carving the night before.

I stepped out onto the porch and froze. The air was fresh and sparkling. The mountain peaks glowed in the sunlight. And the whole gravel parking area was covered with huge black raven feathers, piled nearly an inch thick in some places. It looked as if every black bird in the mountains had shed all its feathers at once. I almost ran back into the cabin. I was suddenly aware that I was more than an hour's drive from the nearest town, with no neighbors to call on if something went wrong. Remoteness is not something you think about in the United States. But I was remote here, and the laws that applied to these mountains were much older than the Union. Eons older.

I drew in a deep breath, went back inside, and took down the loaded rifle. Best not to take chances. I also tucked my cell phone into the pocket that didn't hold the totem. Then I waded through the black feathers until I reached the path down to the river. I heard a deep-throated caw from somewhere above me, but I didn't look up.

The river looked completely ordinary, and I felt my body relax as I lay the rifle down on the bank and waded in. A day of fishing would calm me down nicely. All this superstitious, occult nonsense was for the birds, I thought, and grinned wickedly, wondering if Raven could hear my thoughts. Hour after peaceful hour passed without incident—at least without an occult incident. I caught a couple of nice-size trout and had to throw back a couple more. I stopped for lunch and was entertained by the antics of a couple of squirrels and a blue jay. But nothing more menacing showed itself. Good. Perhaps I'd dreamed the whole crazy thing, I mused, lying back on the bank for a bit of a snooze, pushing thoughts of black feathers out of my mind.

By midafternoon, I was waist-deep in water and getting ready to quit for the day when a heck of a big trout slammed onto my line. It nearly knocked me over. I had to jam my feet between a couple of underwater rocks to retain my balance as the mammoth fish fought with me. This was what I lived for— why I had come to this remote cabin. We dueled for ten, twelve minutes. Then I felt my line come up, and a huge trout leapt out of the water. What a beauty! What a beauty!

At the height of the fish's leap, a huge raven swept down out of nowhere and grabbed the fish in its sharp talons. Flapping mighty black wings, it headed skyward, and suddenly I was playing tug of war with a bird instead of a fish. It was strong— too strong for a mere bird. It pulled me right out of the water, and I was nearly three feet aloft before I let go of my fishing pole and dropped face-first into the river. By the time I clambered to my feet, fish, pole, and bird were gone. And the pocket where I'd tucked the totem pole had turned to ice.

Around me, the woods had gone silent. Sounds I hadn't even been aware of suddenly were not there: the chatter of the squirrels, the chirps and squawks of the birds, the rustle of chipmunks and other small creatures running through the ferns, pine needles, and bracken that littered the ground. All those sounds were missing. The only things I heard were the soft whisper of the breeze and the swish and gurgle of the river. And those sounds were no longer friendly to my ears.

I scrambled for the bank, my right thigh tingling and numb with the cold. Grabbing for rifle, tackle box, and lunch pail, I raced up the path for the cabin. Suddenly, the light was gone—blotted out as if a giant hand had been clapped over the sun. Swirling mist was everywhere, whipping thickly around the trunks and branches of the trees, obscuring everything more than two or three feet around me. And then Coyote came.

Huge—taller than a mountain peak—he came with the mist. In a way, he was part of the mist. I stopped my headlong flight and reared back when I saw the giant figure blocking my path. It was flickering in and out of reality, and I could see it clearly only if I looked out of the corner of my eye. Pricked ears, each taller than a house. A muzzle reaching to the very top of the tall trees lining each side of the river path. The bulk of his gray body filled all available space—giant trees bending and splintering beneath his haunches as he sat down in front of me. A huge paw—big as a truck—came slamming down and knocked me to the ground. I lay under the crushing weight, my face pressed into a pile of dead leaves, my heart beating frantically. I grabbed

the ice-encrusted totem in my pocket and shouted: "Go away!"
And in my mind, a massive voice said: "No!"

Gathering all my strength of will, I pushed mentally at the
giant being. It was wavering in and out of visibility but was
still real enough to crush the breath out of my aching body.
Holding the totem in a hand that burned with cold, I shoved
at the god once, twice. On the third push, the weight on me
lessened. Immediately, I rolled away and ran through the fog,
dodging around the bulk of the being and jumping right over
its enormous tail. It was too huge to turn quickly. I heard trees
toppling as it struggled to its feet.

I dropped everything but the totem pole and ran faster than
I had ever run before. I thought that my heart would come
bursting out of my chest with the effort. I swept out of the
entrance to the pathway and raced through the graveled parking
lot, sending black feathers flying upward in a cloud. Then I was
inside the cabin, slamming the door and driving the bolt home.
Underneath my waders, my frozen pocket warmed and began
to melt. I sagged with relief.

I sank to the floor and sat with my head in my hands until
the dizziness faded and I was sure my legs would hold me. Then
I got up, changed my clothes, and started dinner. A heavy fog
was all around the cabin, causing an early dusk. I desperately
wanted to leave this remote cabin and return to my home in
eastern Washington, but I knew it wouldn't be safe to drive
out there tonight—especially if Coyote was still around. I was
sure that he would be able to crush my little car with one swipe
of the paw that had pinned me to the ground. The soothing
routine of chopping vegetables, peeling potatoes, and cooking
up some ham-steaks (since the fish I'd caught had been left on

the riverbank), soon calmed me—as much as I could be calm with two quasimythical gods angry with me.

It was full night before the mist dissipated. The squashed, orange-colored moon was back and looked closer to full. I made another fire in the wood-burning stove and took out the third book on the occult, determined to discover what the symbols on the totem pole meant. Perhaps they would help me placate Raven and Coyote.

It was almost ten o'clock when I found two of the marks on the totem pole. The man who carved them had borrowed powerful symbols from a completely different religion, which—according to the book—made them more powerful still when combined with his own magic. The first symbol was for binding. The second stood for tying—the image portrayed was that of a cowboy twisting a rope around and around the legs of a prone calf. I gulped, trying to swallow the huge lump in my throat. Little prickles of electricity were running up and down my arms and legs. Did that mean what I thought it meant? Did the black totem pole in some way bind the gods to the person who held it?

The shadows in the corners of the living area seemed suddenly dark and full of menace. On the table under the lamp, the little totem pole frosted over. And outside, a raucous cawing came from many throats. I raced to the window and stared outside in the light of the squashed moon. Black birds were dive-bombing my car, slamming into it with their bodies, running talons along the roof, the hood, the trunk. The whole parking area seethed with black bodies, the moonlight glinting off the sheen of their feathers. My rifle had been abandoned with my tackle and lunch pail on the river path. Anyway, I knew it was useless against this attack. I picked up the frozen totem pole and willed the ravens away from my car. Nothing happened.

Then I heard a thunderous cry, and something massive landed on the roof, shaking the entire house. Dust and ceiling plaster rained down on my head. "Caw! Caw!" Raven's huge voice shook the very earth beneath the cabin, and I toppled onto the rag rug on the floor and scrambled on my hands and knees until I was hidden under the kitchen counter, clutching the frozen totem pole to my chest. My whole body felt numb with terror, and I couldn't think. I just followed my instincts, which told me to hide from the menace outside.

The terrible screeching and cawing and the scraping sound of talons on metal went on for a long time. Then there came a roaring wind as wings wider than a shopping mall flapped against the sky and Raven took off, shaking the house and collapsing a huge chunk of the ceiling.

I crawled my way to the bedroom, leaving all the lights on in the cabin. I pulled myself up onto the bed, knowing that it wasn't over. The totem pole was pulsing with cold. I shoved it to the far side of the bed and pulled the covers over my head, so exhausted by terror that I no longer felt anything at all. Outside, the sounds of the attacking ravens faded away. I closed my eyes and dozed, my mind shutting down in sheer self-defense. I didn't even flinch when the howling began. I heard huge coyotes flinging themselves against the walls of the cabin and pounding against the front and back doors.

Some last vestige of self-preservation made me crawl into the bathroom with the frosty totem pole. The bathroom had no windows and only one door. I pulled a heavy chest of drawers in front of the door, then climbed into the bathtub and fell asleep, resurfacing once when I heard the sound of breaking glass and a second time when I heard sniffing sounds coming from the bottom of the bathroom door. From what seemed—to my dazed mind—like a great distance, I heard a body slam against the bathroom door. It splintered but held firm. Eventually, the slamming stopped, the howls faded away, the totem grew warm, and I fell back into a numbed sleep.

—

I awoke to another sunny morning. The totem was still warm, so I crept from my refuge in the bathroom. I found a devastated cabin. My bedding was ripped apart, foam and springs gushing forth from tears in the mattress. The couches, tables, and chairs in the living room were overturned and ripped. The kitchen table was on its side, the drying plates I'd placed there in shards. A window in the kitchen was broken, and tufts of coyote fur clung to the sharp pieces of glass on the floor. Surprisingly, the spare bedrooms were fine. I guess the coyotes could smell which rooms I'd been using.

I cleaned up as best I could, still numb from the terror of the previous night. I didn't know what to do. If the symbols in the old books were accurate, then Coyote and Raven would probably kill me if I didn't find a way of negating the binding that the totem pole had upon them. The only thing I could think to do was to show the totem to Joe, a buddy of mine who was studying to be a medicine man. Maybe he'd be able to tell me how to break the spell.

I peeked cautiously out the window of the cabin before emerging with my bags and fishing poles. The coast was clear. I only hoped my poor, damaged car would hold together long enough for me to make it to Joe's home. The claw marks scarring the hood were almost an inch deep in places, but they were nothing compared to the huge chunks torn out of the roof of the cabin by the massive talons of Raven.

As I drove off with a squeal of tires, black feathers cascading everywhere, I glanced into the rearview mirror and saw a massive coyote—big as a black bear—standing in the center of the clearing, glaring after me. I gulped and hit the gas.

All the way down the mountain, black birds followed my car, sometimes diving straight toward my windshield. After the first attack, when I swerved and almost ran off the road, I ignored them and kept my eyes fixed on the center line.

I rattled into Joe's driveway about dinnertime, praying that he would be home. I'd flinched every time I saw a black bird in the sky on the drive, and that had been more often than was comfortable. Someone was watching me, I knew. And I didn't like it one bit.

Fortunately, Joe was home and answered the door on the first ring. He took one look at my face and hauled me inside without questions. A minute later, I was sitting at his kitchen table and his wife—a lovely lady named Emma—was pouring me a beer.

"What happened?" Joe asked, after I'd had a few sips of beer to calm my shaking nerves. I told him everything—from the moment I'd seen the black carving in the box to the black birds that followed my car all the way to his house. I pointed toward his window, knowing what was out there without even bothering to look. The coldness of the totem was throbbing through the leather bag that lay against my leg.

Joe and Emma looked out the window, straight into the beady black eyes of Raven, who was perched on the railing of the back deck. He fluffed his black feathers until he was twice his normal size—which was already enormous. Then he flapped away with an impudent "caw," leaving claw marks etched deep into the wood.

"Good Lord," Joe breathed. He muttered something in his native tongue, lifting his hand in a gesture of power, or possibly warding. "You'd better show me this carving," he added, turning back to me, his face creased with worry.

"It's all yours," I said, picking up the leather bag. The coldness had faded with the departure of Raven, so I figured it was safe to touch the carving. I placed it on the table between us, and Joe drew in a sharp breath. This afternoon, the strange carvings and symbols writhed and twisted as if they were alive. It made my eyes water just to look at them. The whole totem pole was wrapped in a glittering haze, as if it were a desert mirage.

Emma gasped when she saw it and retreated to the kitchen counter, as far away as she could get without leaving the room. As for Joe—he reeled back in his chair as if someone had slapped him. "Smudge," he gasped to his wife. She nodded and left the room. A moment later she returned from Joe's study with a couple of smudge sticks—wands made of the leaves of a plant or a mixture of plants, tied together and dried.

Joe lit the end of each wand then extinguished the flames once they were smoldering. First he smudged the room, carrying the lit stick clockwise, being careful to blow smoke into corners and behind doors. Motioning me away from the table, he blew the smoke all over the surface of the table and over the black carving. Then he had me stand facing him and passed the smoking wand back and forth, starting at my feet and moving upward, with special attention to the region of my heart. When

TOTEM

he reach my head, he had me turn clockwise, and he passed the wand down my back.

As the scented smoke whirled around me, I felt a lessening of the stress and tension that had gripped me from the moment I first picked up the carved totem pole. I still felt its presence in my mind, tugging at me like a dog stripping a bone. But its impact had lessened. On the table, the air around the carving was no longer shimmering.

Eventually, Joe sat back down at the table with the smoldering smudge sticks in a jar between him and the carving. He refused to touch the totem pole, but he leaned closer to stare at it for a long time.

"This is a binding," he said at last. "A very old, very powerful binding. But it is not Native American in origin. This totem was made by a black magician from your people, my friend. Somehow, he learned some of the secret teachings of the local tribes and he combined their ancient secrets with his own black arts to give him power. I think he must have practiced a form of ancient European mysticism. Those terrible faces you could not recognize—I think they are demons from that tradition. As are these symbols . . . " Joe shuddered and leaned back into the smoke from the smudge sticks. He drew in a deep breath of the scented herbs, which seemed to calm him. "This is very bad medicine, my friend. It traps part of the spirits of Raven and Coyote within the wood, making them do the bidding of the man who wields the carving—if he is a powerful enough magician. As soon as you picked up the totem, you caught the attention of the gods. And because you are neither a magician yourself—as the grandfather of the girl at the garage sale must have been—nor a member of a magician's family—which also offers a measure of protection—Raven and Coyote were able to turn the magic of the carving against you."

I drew in a shaky breath. I had suspected something like this.

"What do I do?" I asked.

"Get rid of it," Joe said promptly. "Destroy it and break the binding upon Raven and Coyote. If it were me, I'd weigh it down and throw it into the Palouse Falls out near Spokane. After doing the proper ceremonies, of course. And when you're done, come back here and I'll give you another smudging. You're gonna need it."

Yes, I was.

—

As I drove through the alternating grasslands and cultivated fields that characterized the Channeled Scablands, where Palouse Falls lay, I pondered the prayers and ceremonies that Joe had taught me for the occasion. Would they work? I hadn't seen a single raven since leaving Joe's place this morning, and neither hide nor hair of a coyote. This itself seemed strange, after so many days of being haunted by one or the other. Could they sense my good intentions? Did they know I sought to free them—and myself—from the dead magician's spell?

I put on my blinker and made the turn onto the road leading to the falls. As I did, a coyote raced out of the cow pasture to my right, ran across the road, slipped under a low fence, and sauntered up the hill on my left. The coyote paused halfway up the slope and turned to look at me with an unmistakably sly expression.

My heart started slamming against my ribs, and I slowed the car and pulled over to the edge of the road, my eyes locked on the coyote's. It had the most . . . human . . . stare. Above it, I heard a raucous caw, and a huge raven swooped down and perched on the blasted remains of a lightning-struck tree a few yards from the meadow where the coyote stood, nearly waist-deep in bluebunch wheatgrass.

Prickles were running up and down my arms and legs as I slowly got out of the car, the carving in my hand. This was the first time I was seeing both a coyote and a raven together. It seemed . . . symbolic.

My gaze never left that of the coyote as my fingers gripped the totem pole, feeling the sharp beak of Raven and rough nose of Coyote. And suddenly, I knew what to do. Drawing my arm back, I threw the totem as far as I could up the hill toward the coyote. It landed on a flat rock a few feet from the creature, which didn't stir at all. In that moment, I would have staked my life on the true identity of the creature—of the god—standing there.

Coyote continued to hold my gaze for a few seconds longer than was comfortable. In that gaze, I felt the weight of the whole land bearing down upon me, and with it came a vision of the past. Coyote was as old as these hills and could remember a time when this land was completely different. He remembered the glaciers creeping down from the north. He had watched the ice damming the great rivers, forming massive lakes larger than the Great Lakes themselves. He'd seen those ice dams break, draining a lake that was more than two thousand feet deep within forty-eight hours. He'd watched the flood waters rip this land to pieces, creating gorges and coulees and waterfalls three times the size of Niagara. And he'd watched the waters drain away and life begin anew in this high desert. Coyote had seen all of this, and much, much more. How dare I, a mere human, command one such as he?

I broke into a sweat, wondering if I had done enough. Throwing the carving to Coyote had seemed like the right thing to do. I had followed my instincts instead of Joe's careful ceremonies. Would it be enough?

Suddenly, Coyote lowered his gaze. He trotted forward, picked up the totem in his mouth, and galloped away up the hill and over the ridge. On the lightning-blasted tree, Raven gave a second mighty caw and flapped up and up into the endless blue sky over the Channeled Scablands.

And then they were gone. And with them passed the shadow of the long-dead magician. The curse was over at last.

Resources

Asfar, Daniel. *Ghost Stories of America*. Edmonton, AB: Ghost House Books, 2001.

Athena. *Ghosts of Seattle*. Atglen, PA: Schiffer Publishing, Ltd., 2007.

Bader, Chris. *Strange Northwest*. Blaine, WA: Hancock House Publishers, 1995.

Battle, Kemp P. *Great American Folklore*. New York: Doubleday & Company, Inc., 1986.

Botkin, B. A., ed. *A Treasury of American Folklore*. New York: Crown, 1944.

Brewer, J. Mason. *American Negro Folklore*. Chicago, IL: Quadrangle Books, 1972.

Brunvand, Jan Harold. *The Choking Doberman and Other Urban Legends*. New York: W. W. Norton, 1984.

———. *The Vanishing Hitchhiker*. New York: W. W. Norton, 1981.

Clark, Ella E. *Indian Legends of the Pacific Northwest*. Berkley and Los Angeles, CA: University of California Press, 1953.

Coffin, Tristram P., and Hennig Cohen, eds. *Folklore in America*. New York: Doubleday & AMP, 1966.

———. *Folklore from the Working Folk of America*. New York: Doubleday, 1973.

Cohen, Daniel, and Susan Cohen. *Hauntings & Horrors*. New York: Dutton Children's Books, 2002.

Costopoulos, Nina. *Lighthouse Ghosts and Legends*. Birmingham, AL: Crane Hill Publishers, 2003.

Davis, Jeff, and Al Eufrasio. *Weird Washington*. New York: Sterling Publishing Co., Inc., 2008.

Davis, Jefferson. *Ghosts and Strange Critters of Washington and Oregon*. Arkansas Vancouver, WA: Norseman Ventures, 1999.

———. *Ghosts, Critters & Sacred Places of Washington and Oregon*. Arkansas Vancouver, WA: Norseman Ventures, 1999.

———. *Ghosts, Critters & Sacred Places of Washington and Oregon II*. Arkansas Vancouver, WA: Norseman Ventures, 2000.

———. *Ghosts, Critters & Sacred Places of Washington and Oregon III*. Arkansas Vancouver, WA: Norseman Ventures, 2005.

Deviny, John. *Exploring Washington's Backroads*. Olympia, WA: Wilder Productions, 2005.

Dorson, R. M. *America in Legend*. New York: Pantheon Books, 1973.

Downer, Deborah L. *Classic American Ghost Stories*. Little Rock, AR: August House Publishers, Inc.

Dwyer, Jeff. *Ghost Hunter's Guide to Seattle and Puget Sound*. Gretna, LA: Pelican Publishing Company, Inc., 2008.

Editors of *Life*. *The Life Treasury of American Folklore*. New York: Time Inc., 1961.

Elizabeth, Norma, and Bruce Roberts. *Lighthouse Ghosts*. Birmingham, AL: Crane Hill Publishers, 1999.

Erdoes, Richard, and Alfonso Ortiz. *American Indian Myths and Legends*. New York: Pantheon Books, 1984.

Flanagan, J. T., and A. P. Hudson. *The American Folk Reader*. New York: A. S. Barnes & Co., 1958.

Garrett, Anita Melanie. *Islands There Were*. Friday Harbor, WA: Long House Printcrafters, 1976.

Hauck, Dennis William. *Haunted Places: The National Directory.* New York: Penguin Books, 1994.

Jameson, W. C. *Buried Treasures of the Pacific Northwest.* Little Rock, AR: August House, Inc., 1995.

Judson, Katherine Berry. *Myths and Legends of the Pacific Northwest: Especially of Washington and Oregon.* Chicago, IL: A. C. McClurg & Co., 1912.

Leach, M. *The Rainbow Book of American Folk Tales and Legends.* New York: The World Publishing Co., 1958.

Leeming, David, and Jake Pagey. *Myths, Legends, & Folktales of America.* New York: Oxford University Press, 1999.

MacDonald, Margaret Reed. *Ghost Stories from the Pacific Northwest.* Little Rock, AR: August House, Inc., 1995.

Mourning Dove. *Coyote Stories.* Caldwell, Idaho: The Caxton Printers, Ltd., 1933.

Murphy, Dan. *Oregon Trail, Voyage of Discovery: The Story Behind the Scenery.* Las Vegas, NV: KC Publications, Inc., 1997.

Norman, Michael, and Beth Scott. *Historic Haunted America.* New York: Tor Books, 1995.

Peck, Catherine, ed. *A Treasury of North American Folk Tales.* New York: W. W. Norton, 1998.

Polley, J., ed. *American Folklore and Legend.* New York: Reader's Digest Association, 1978.

Ramsey, Jarold, ed. *Coyote Was Going There.* Seattle, WA: University of Washington Press, 1977.

Reevy, Tony. *Ghost Train!* Lynchburg, VA: TLC Publishing, 1998.

Richardson, David. *Pig War Islands.* Eastsound, WA: Orcas Publishing Company, 1990.

Rule, Leslie. *Coast to Coast Ghosts*. Kansas City, KS: Andrews McMeel Publishing, 2001.

Salmonson, Jessica Amanda. *The Mysterious Doom and Other Ghostly Tales of the Pacific Northwest*. Seattle, WA: Sasquatch Books, 1992.

———. *Phantom Waters: Northwest Legends of Rivers, Lakes, and Shores*. Seattle, WA: Sasquatch Books, 1995.

Schwartz, Alvin. *Scary Stories to Tell in the Dark*. New York: Harper Collins, 1981.

Seaburg, William R., and Pamela T. Amoss, eds. *Badger and Coyote Were Neighbors*. Corvallis, OR: Oregon State University Press, 2000.

Skinner, Charles M. *American Myths and Legends, Vol. 1*. Philadelphia: J. B. Lippincott, 1903.

———. *Myths and Legends of Our Own Land, Vols. 1 & 2*. Philadelphia, PA: J. B. Lippincott, 1896.

Smith, Barbara. *Ghost Stories of Washington*. Auburn, WA: Lone Pine Publishing, 2000.

Spence, Lewis. *North American Indians: Myths and Legends Series*. London: Bracken Books, 1985.

Students of Haskell Institute. *Myths, Legends, and Superstitions of North American Indian Tribes*. Cherokee, NC: Cherokee Publications, 1995.

Walls, Robert E., ed. *Bibliography of Washington State Folklore and Folklife*. Seattle, WA: University of Washington Press, 1987.

Zeitlin, Steven J., Amy J. Kotkin, and Holly Cutting Baker. *A Celebration of American Family Folklore*. New York: Pantheon Books, 1982.

From *Spooky Virginia,*
also now available from GPP

Shower of Stones

NEWPORT

I don't reckon folks will believe the story I've got to tell. But I swear on a stack of Bibles that it's the truth, so help me God. I was a slave back in them days, working for Doc McChesney on his plantation-farm called Greenwood. I was working as a kitchen assistant and general housemaid when the troubles began. And they were amazing troubles, let me tell you.

It all started with a young slave gal named Maria. We heard her screaming something awful out in the yard. A minute later she came running into the parlor where Missus McChesney was rocking the baby. Maria was cryin' her eyes out, and her teeth were chattering with fear. She looked terrible, with welts and bruises all over. When we asked her how she got all beat up, she claimed an old woman had appeared in the yard and started beating on her. The old woman had chased her right up to the house; she just barely got away. Poor Maria could barely speak, she was so afraid.

A bunch of us went running out into the yard armed with rolling pins and brooms and such, ready to do battle with the old woman. But no one was there. We searched all the outbuildings and found nothing.

But that weren't nothing compared to what happened next. I was walking through the yard one, maybe two days later when a huge chunk of mud came hurling toward me out of nowhere. Hit me square in the chest and just about ruined my best shirt. Furious, I started shouting and looking around for the culprit. But I was alone in the yard. My yells brought the mistress of the house to the door, and we both saw—swear to God—two more huge clumps of mud rise up off the ground and propel themselves across the yard. I had to duck to avoid getting more mud on my shirt. The mistress was staring with her mouth open in shock. She beckoned to me to run into the house quick. I didn't need telling twice. I was across the yard lickety-split, and I heard two more mud clots hit the kitchen door just after I slammed it shut.

Inside the house, Cook told me that someone—or rather something—had been throwing sizzling hot rocks. The rocks had already knocked over a pitcher full of water, broken a vase of flowers, and put some mighty big dents in the furniture.

We were all afraid of the ghost or phantom or whatever it was throwing mud and rocks around. Over the next few days, it really got active. We all had to duck more than once when objects came flying out of nowhere, but the spirit seemed particularly attentive to little Maria. She'd be working quietly at the kitchen table or dusting in the parlor when all at once she'd start shrieking and crying and fall right on the floor. She said something was beating on her. We could all hear the spirit slapping her, and we all saw bruises and welts forming on her face and arms out of nowhere.

First time it happened, I ran forward and tried to stop the creature, but it gave me such a slap that I flew backward and rolled head over heels, landing with a bang at the feet of the mistress, who'd just come in the door. After that, she told us to stay away from Maria if we saw the spirit pummeling her. She didn't want anyone else getting hurt by the phantom.

The doctor thought the whole thing was nonsense. He said Maria was just pretending in order to get attention, and he blamed the rock and mud throwing on hoodlums.

But things got even worse. Whole showers of stones started raining down on the roof. Sounded just like rapid gunfire the first time it happened. We thought we were under attack by marauders, and a bunch of us crowded underneath the kitchen table, quaking with fear. After the shower of stones had stopped, we ventured outside to see the damage. The yard was littered with rocks the size of a man's fist. That first shower of stones happened after dark, but it wasn't long before they were coming in daylight too.

It puzzled me how the doctor could blame the attacks on hoodlums. Anyone brave enough to venture outside when the rocks started flyin' could see that there wasn't anyone there to throw them. It wasn't always showers. Sometimes just one or two rocks came hurling out of the sky. Some of those rocks were big! They weighed too much to be tossed about by an ordinary fellow, not even the blacksmith.

All these supernatural happenings soon caught the attention of folks in the nearby towns. Folks started trespassing on our property, hoping to see the Devil's handiwork for themselves.

It made Doctor McChesney furious to have all those strangers lurking about. At first it was just a few folks from the nearby regions. But word spread, and hundreds of folks began traveling from all over to see the stone showers at the farm. The doctor quickly abandoned his usual courtesy toward strangers and drove curiosity-seekers away with such yelling and cursing that they fled the property as fast as they could. Some of them swore they'd seen the Devil himself on the farm and told everyone they'd barely escaped with their lives. But what they'd really seen was the doctor in a rage.

'Course, when a wagonload of church elders arrived, the doctor and his missus welcomed them politely and invited them to stay for dinner. Oh my, we enjoyed seeing the look on their faces when a sharp black stone came flying down from the ceiling and cut one of their biscuits clean in half. They were amazed, frightened too. Never saw folks exit a house so quick after a meal, and with the barest courtesies. I'd have been indignant on behalf of my master and mistress if I hadn't found it so funny.

That evening Mrs. McChesney started beggin' her husband to move away from the devil-ridden house. Of course the doctor refused. In spite of the almost daily stone showers and the mud flinging and Maria's beatings, he still maintained that nothing was wrong at Greenwood. But the mistress was convinced that the Devil was behind the incidents at the farm and that he would keep plaguing them until they left the premises or until Maria— who seemed to be the main target of the attacks—was sent away.

A few days after the elders' visit, Maria was outside on the porch pouting on account of Cook wouldn't give her a snack when a bunch of floppy round circles appeared out of nowhere and pummeled her from all sides. I saw the whole

thing through the open kitchen door and let out a yell. Cook
and me and some of the McChesney children ran out onto the
porch and stared at Maria, who was covered with pancakes!
That'll teach her to snack before dinner!

Then the spirit started plaguing the McChesney baby. And
I didn't find that funny at all. Little James was lying in his cradle
when he suddenly began crying and tossing about like a mad
thing. I was making beds upstairs when I heard him scream out.
When both his mama and I ran into the room to check on him,
we saw him rolling about wildly as tiny red pinpricks of blood
appeared all over his little body. We screamed for the doctor.

"I want that girl sent away right now!" Missus McChesney
said to her husband once the baby settled down a bit. She was
in such a frenzy that the doctor reluctantly agreed to send Maria
to stay at the home of his brother-in-law.

Maria left the next mornin' with a small satchel of clothes
and some food to eat on the long walk. All that day, the house
was plumb quiet. No stones hit the roof; no mud flew through
the yard. And the red pinpricks disappeared like magic from
baby James. Everything was so peaceful and still, we couldn't
believe it. Then Maria came walking back into the yard late in
the evening. Almost at once, a big ol' rock crashed into the
roof of the house.

Everyone was so surprised to see her! We crowded out
onto the porch, demanding to know why she'd come on back.
She told us that the spirit had followed her to the other house.
As soon as Maria came in sight of the brother-in-law's place,
she heard a sound like the galloping of a dozen horses. The
family all rushed into the house and found every darned stick
of furniture piled up in the center of the floor! Rocks and clods

SHOWER OF STONES

of mud appeared out of thin air and hurled themselves at them too. Just then the doctor's brother-in-law saw Maria through the parlor window. He yelled at her to go back home at once, which she did. She had nowhere else to go.

I saw the look on the mistress's face when she heard Maria's story. She was terrible afraid. But what could she do? Her husband wouldn't move away or sell Maria. He didn't believe anything was wrong at Greenwood.

Things got real bad after Maria's return. That terrible spirit beat her almost daily, and the showers of rocks battered the roof nearly to pieces. Stones and clots of mud hurled themselves randomly inside the house. They came from every which way—ceiling, floor, walls! And the yard was no safer than the house.

Doctor McChesney saw all them things happening and still refused to believe that an evil spirit had invaded the house.

And then the baby got worse. Little James suffered repeatedly from seizures, and the pinpricks reappeared on his body. His convulsions grew so bad that his mother could barely hold him. Once while Mrs. McChesney rocked little James, a chair walked itself across the room and stopped beside her as if it wanted to look at the baby in her arms. She ran to the far side of the room, and that darned chair followed her. With a scream of terror, she ran clean out of the house and wouldn't come back inside until her husband came home.

The doctor still refused to leave Greenwood or to send Maria away. He insisted nothing was really wrong at the farm. He wouldn't even ask the local church for help, which was downright foolish to my way of thinkin'. If anyone could exorcise that evil spirit, it was the pastor of the church.

But the doctor wouldn't hear of it. He insisted that his little boy was suffering from a curable disease, not from some evil haunt. Day and night, while rocks and mud clots pummeled the house and yard, the doctor dosed the poor little fellow with medicine and tried everything he knew to cure him from the seizures. But they just got worse and worse until his little body was constantly aflame with bloody red pinpricks.

Then, in the middle of a terrible convulsion, little James died. And there weren't nothin' his daddy could do to save him.

Missus McChesney wept and wept when her son died. After that, she sat in silence, rocking in her chair as stones showered down on the roof of the house and rocks hurled themselves about inside. Her silence was even more terrible than her tears.

Finally, she told the doctor that she was leaving. He could go or stay as he pleased, but she and the children were done with this evil place. I peered cautiously through the open parlor door to see what the doctor would do. His face was full of deep, sad lines that hadn't been there before little James's death, and his broad shoulders were slumped in defeat. In that moment, he finally admitted—to himself as well as his wife—that something evil had taken over Greenwood.

"Please don't leave," the doctor begged his wife. "I will sell the girl and her parents, if only you will stay here with me."

Missus McChesney closed her eyes for a minute, as if she was in pain. And then she agreed.

Within a few days, Maria and her parents were sold and left Greenwood forever. From the moment Maria left the plantation, the showers of stone ceased.

About the Author

S. E. Schlosser has been telling stories since she was a child, when games of "let's pretend" quickly built themselves into full-length tales acted out with friends. A graduate of Houghton College, the Institute of Children's Literature, and Rutgers University, she created and maintains the award-winning Web site Americanfolklore.net, where she shares a wealth of stories from all fifty states, some dating back to the origins of America. Sandy spends much of her time answering questions from visitors to the site. Many of her favorite e-mails come from other folklorists who delight in practicing the old tradition of who can tell the tallest tale.

About the Illustrator

Artist Paul Hoffman trained in painting and printmaking, with his first extensive illustration work on assignment in Egypt, drawing ancient wall reliefs for the University of Chicago. His work graces books of many genres—children's titles, textbooks, short story collections, natural history volumes, and numerous cookbooks. For *Spooky Washington,* he employed a scratchboard technique and an active imagination.